STEALTH
BOMBER

Invisible warplane, black budget

Bill Sweetman

Motorbooks International
Publishers & Wholesalers Inc
Osceola, Wisconsin 54020, USA ®

First published in 1989 by Motorbooks
International Publishers & Wholesalers Inc,
P O Box 2, 729 Prospect Avenue, Osceola,
WI 54020 USA

Motorbooks International is a certified
trademark, registered with the United
States Patent Office

Printed and bound in the United States of
America

**Library of Congress Cataloging-in-
Publication Data**
Sweetman, Bill
   Stealth bomber.

   1. B-2 bomber. I. Title.
UG1242.B6S95 1989   358.4'2   88-33046
ISBN 0-87938-346-1

The cover photo was taken by Bill
Sweetman at the roll-out of the first B-2, on
November 22, 1988. *The back cover*
illustration depicts a hypothetical internal
configuration of the aircraft. *The photo on
the rear flap* was supplied by John W.
Alexanders/Sky Films.

Contents

For Martin and Evan, in hope that every B-2, B-52 and B-1 will, one day, rest and rust in the Arizona desert

Acknowledgments

There is no way to list all the people who have, in one way or another, helped in the preparation of this book. Particular thanks, though, to all those who responded to requests for illustrations (usually at the last minute) including Jay Miller, Mike Badrocke, Chuck Hansen, Ramon Lopez, Terry Clawson, Pete Dakan and Roy Lange.

Thanks to the efficient and friendly Motorbooks staff: Tim Parker, Barbara Harold, Greg Field and the rest.

And above all, thanks to Mary Pat, who can now write her own book on living with the the obsessive personality.

Foreword

People often ask me about my sources, then refuse to believe me when I reply that everything I look for is to be found in books. This is such a book.

Bill Sweetman is a genius at finding things out, but far more so in his ability to take a few facts and find their place in a coherent picture. I call this game "connect the dots," though a more apt analogy is a jigsaw puzzle. Taking a few facts that you do know, and realizing that somehow the facts are interconnected, your job is to determine how the pieces relate to one another. If you do the job right, you can deduce facts that you do not have—the ones which you cannot find out without earning attention from some very serious people not known for their sense of humor. These people are called security officers.

Some will criticize Bill for writing on so sensitive a subject as Stealth. I've had the same problem myself. But we live in a free society where government policy is formulated, at least indirectly, through the consent of the governed. On technically complex issues, this can be a difficult thing to accomplish. The American people know, for example, that nuclear war is something we want to avoid—the question is, How?

All too often government officials tell us that they *can't* tell us why they do certain things. Those who oppose the government's policy seize on that to say that it's all lies, that it will never work, and that it will make the world more dangerous, not less so. "Defense experts" on both sides will debate issues without substantive discussion of what exactly they're talking about. This leaves the citizen with a choice between blind faith in words of a government spokesman or the monotonous and politically motivated ranting of a professional naysayer.

The general press, instead of lighting candles in the darkness, merely adds smoke because its members too often lack the scientific expertise to discuss or even investigate an increasingly technical world. As a result, we get thirty column inches of back-room chatter on cost overruns and third-hand analysis spoon-fed by anonymous sources with unreported political agendas of their own: lots of sound and fury, signifying not very much.

Today, issues tend to replace facts, but in the proper scheme of things, issues are formed by facts and then shaped by principles into coherent public policy upon which the society as a whole can agree.

The value of this book is that it traces the history of a not-so-mysterious trend in military strategy—Stealth—and shows how it will affect future strategy. The revolutionary Minuteman used stealth—hiding behind a log to ambush his red-coated adversary—and had learned stealth the hard way, from the first Americans. Stealth came to armies in the institutional sense in the late nineteenth century, when rifled musketry made bright uniforms too dangerous to wear, and blending in with the background became the difference between life and death. Warships changed their paint scheme from white to gray for the same reason at the turn of the century, and the scarlet triplane of the Red Baron was a short-lived, and possibly fatal extravagance. "The tallest tree," says the Chinese proverb, "is the first to be cut down." On the battlefield, it does not pay to advertise.

Stealth technology, Bill tells us, has changed the rules of military strategy, but not the principle—and suddenly an immensely complex series of questions becomes comprehensible.

Bill Sweetman tells us how this most complex and expensive of aircraft fits into a continuing theme of military history. The name of the game is not war fighting, but war *prevention*. The paradox, also borne out by history, is that being ready to fight a war is the surest way of preventing one.

The importance of the Stealth bomber is that it hugely complicates the task of an adversary. To defend against it will compel him to spend vast sums of money on defensive measures that might otherwise be spent on offensive ones. Development of Stealth technology is a sensible and potentially vital aspect of national defense. By its very existence, the B-2 makes America a safer place.

In tracing the history of the concept, and its integration into current planning, Bill Sweetman does our country a great service. He makes the complex, if not simple, then at least, comprehensible. Those who read this book will understand why some feel this technology to be desirable. Whether they decide to support the B-2 or not is beside the point. They will have enough information to make an informed judgment. That is why we have a free press, and one reason we have armed forces is to protect it.

Tom Clancy

Hunt for Red October (Naval Institute Press)
Red Storm Rising (Putnam)
Patriot Games (Putnam)
Cardinal of the Kremlin (Putnam)

Chapter 1

The survivable bomber

The bomber will always get through.

Stanley Baldwin, former Prime Minister of Britain, in November 1932

Bombers are for fighting nuclear wars. Before the nuclear age, bombers symbolized both the strength of airpower and the terror of warfare: remember Picasso's *Guernica*. The bomber's crew, meticulously destroying the targets, killing enemies and victims that they never saw, epitomized faceless military force. While the atomic bomb multiplied the destructiveness of the bomber by several orders of magnitude, it did not radically change bomber doctrine. What bombers are intended to do, and how they accomplish their missions, are aspects of this doctrine which have gradually evolved since the earliest days of military aviation.

The bomber has survived many attempts to consign it to the world's aeronautical museums. It might have been hard to find one opinion which Robert S. McNamara and Nikita Khrushchev held in common; but, in 1961, President Kennedy's new Secretary of Defense and the General Secretary of the Soviet Communist Party would certainly have agreed that the bomber was obsolete. No conceivable aircraft could survive a flight of thousands of miles through a lethal thicket of radars, missiles and fighters, coordinated by powerful computers. All the bomber's missions would ultimately be taken over by automated long-range missiles, fired from submarines or the hardened concrete-and-steel pits called silos.

Neither man expected that Californians, New Yorkers, Georgians and Russians not yet born could grow up, enlist in their air forces and learn to fly and operate new strategic bombers, nor that the new aircraft would serve alongside the very machines that McNamara and Khrushchev planned to scrap in 1961. The bomber has proved to be more "survivable" than the experts could have dreamed.

On November 22, 1988, a group of 500 people gathered at Palmdale, California. After careful security checks,

Northrop's B-2 rolls out at Palmdale, California, on November 22, 1988, welcomed by Thomas V. Jones (standing), Northrop's chairman and chief executive officer. Also present (seated from left to right) are USAF

Secretary Edward C. Aldridge, USAF Chief of Staff General Larry Welch and Brigadier General Richard Scofield, director of the B-2 program office. USAF

they were driven in vans to a site where temporary bleachers had been erected, facing a low, sandy-beige hangar. Just before noon, the hangar doors slowly opened; a USAF-issue tractor coughed to life and, as though it were dragging some strange sea creature from its lair, pulled an extraordinary airplane into the sunlight. For the first time, the Northrop B-2 Advanced Technology Bomber appeared in public view.

The B-2 is the spearhead of a revolution in airpower, but at the same time it embodies themes which run throughout the development of the bomber and underlie all the changes made possible by advances in aircraft and weapon technology. One of these is survivability. If the bomber is destroyed or is forced to abandon its mission, it has been defeated. The other thread of bomber development concerns navigation and weapon-aiming; if the bomber cannot find or hit its target, it has failed just as completely as if it had been shot down. Compared with survivability and navigation, even such issues as speed and payload are of secondary importance.

The first bombers

The first bombing raids to be directed against centers of population and production, rather than at opposing military formations, were made in the first half of 1915 by German airships. The campaign peaked in 1916, when Zeppelin and Schutte-Lanz airships took part in eight large-scale raids on London, the largest of which involved sixteen of the giant craft. With such a slow and steady platform, nautical navigation techniques ensured sufficient accuracy to hit an area target such as a city.

Some of the later Zeppelins featured a unique bad-weather bombing aid: a small, streamlined nacelle called a "cloud car," accommodating an observer and a telephone. The cloud car could be lowered below the cloudbase on a long cable, so that the observer could search for targets while the airship remained concealed.

Frightening as they were to the civilian population, airships could not survive over enemy territory. They were big, slow and easy to hit, and when they were hit they burned, being filled with hydrogen. Airship raids continued into 1918, with the chances of survival diminishing to near-suicidal levels, but long before that time the bomber airplane had assumed the primary responsibility for strategic attacks. In June 1917, for example, a formation of fourteen Gotha G-type bombers attacked London in daylight, killing 162 people and injuring

Gotha bombers such as this aircraft were the first airplanes to attack cities in the enemy's homeland, starting in 1917. Jay Miller/ Aerofax

462. In January 1918, a single Staaken R-type bomber, the largest airplane of its day, dropped a 660 pound bomb which killed thirty-eight people in a London printing works. Much smaller and faster than the airships, the bombers were far more difficult to catch, and escaped with minimal losses. The result was an outraged call for improved defenses and immediate retaliation.

Bombing strategy development

Although these raids achieved little in military terms, apart from causing some guns and fighter squadrons to be held back from the Western front, they inspired a few officers to advocate a new form of warfare, using long-range aircraft to strike cities and production centers, destroying an enemy nation's ability and will to wage war. The advocates of bombing included the US Army's General Billy Mitchell; Sir Hugh Trenchard,

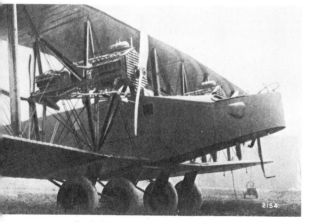

Led by bomber advocate Sir Hugh Trenchard, the Royal Air Force planned to retaliate for raids on London by bombing Berlin with the long-range Handley Page V/1500. The 1914-18 war ended before it was ready. Jay Miller/Aerofax

who assumed command of the new Royal Air Force (RAF) in April 1918, marking the first time that an air force had won equal footing with the Army and Navy; and Italy's General Giulo Douhet. Mitchell used his bombers to sink a number of old German battleships in trials in 1921, before his determination and combative ways led to the end of his service career. Trenchard, nicknamed "Boom" because of his enthusiasm for the bomber, concentrated the postwar RAF's budget on bombers, while Douhet's book, *The Command of the Air*, predicted that airpower would be the deciding factor in future wars and became a best-seller among works on military theory.

By the early thirties, there were increasing calls for the development, production and use of bombers to be controlled or even banned by international agreement. Douhet's prophecies had permeated the consciousness of the public, which now feared bombers as people today fear nuclear weapons. A British politician and former Prime Minister, Stanley Baldwin, campaigned for aerial disarmament. "The man in the street," should realize, he said in November 1932, "that there is no power on earth that can prevent him from being bombed . . . the bomber will always get through."

At the time, this was almost the case, particularly for a small country such as Britain, in close proximity to its likely enemies. Flying at high altitude, bombers were inaudible and almost invisible from the ground, and the only way to intercept them was for fighters to take off as they passed overhead, track them visually and overtake them. At night or in bad weather, this would be almost impossible, and elite bomber crews frequently demonstrated their ability to navigate using compass, sextant and clock, without reference to the ground, and still find their targets.

Radar and navigation

Radar and reality changed everything. Developed independently and concurrently in Britain and Germany, radar gave the defenders time to prepare for a raid, and told them from which direction it would come. From then on, controllers in quiet, well-protected bunkers could track the raid and guide the fighters into position for an attack by radio. The bomber's speed and advantage of surprise were thereby negated.

Reality took a hand in genuine bombing exercises, as opposed to navigation demonstrations, where average crews were sent off to find unfamiliar targets at night. Between 1937 and 1939, no fewer than 478 of RAF Bomber Command's crews forcelanded after getting lost at night, over a familiar country spangled with the lights of peacetime. One officer recalled later that the results

The US Army Air Force planned to fight its way to its targets in daylight, relying on massed guns for protection. Eventually, the *weight of guns, turrets, gunners and ammunition on aircraft like this B-17G far exceeded their bombloads.* Boeing

of occasional bombing trials "should have depressed us more than they did." The average crew, it was found, could be expected to get within fifty miles of the target without ground references such as lights or outside aid.

Daylight bombing

The link between navigation and survivability was made in the prewar years. The US Army Air Corps, recognizing that night navigation was unsatisfactory, resolved to bomb in daylight;

Bomber Command also realized that such operations might be necessary. To give their crews some chance of survival, both services ordered bigger, faster bombers which could carry many defensive machine guns as well as a heavy bombload. The first of these to appear, the Boeing B-17, was considered so well protected that it was dubbed the Flying Fortress. It was followed into service by the Consolidated B-24 Liberator, while Britain produced such heavy bombers

The Consolidated B-24J Liberator mounted four fully powered turrets, each with two .50 caliber machine guns, plus two manually aimed guns at the waist position. It had a larger bombload than the B-17G, but was considered much more vulnerable to battle damage. Jay Miller/Aerofax

as the Avro Lancaster and the Handley Page Halifax. Germany produced no such aircraft in quantity before 1942, and in daylight raids on London, in the summer of 1940, its lightly defended bombers were shot down in swarms despite being escorted by fighters.

In 1942, as US war production accelerated, and as British heavy bombers entered service in increasing numbers, RAF Bomber Command and the US 8th Air Force prepared their air offensive against Germany. Talk of a "round-the-clock joint offensive" was an ingenious cover story. In fact, the US and British bomber doctrines were diametrically opposed, and many members of each service thought the other was wasting its time.

US Army Air Force (USAAF) doctrine called for precision attacks, mainly on factories producing weapons or vital components. The only way to hit such targets was in daylight visual conditions, from a straight, level bombing run which allowed the bombardier to work out an accurate release point. The bombers were sitting ducks for fighters, their contrails visible from hundreds of miles away. In an attempt to beat off the fighters, the USAAF added more, heavier guns to its bombers, replacing .30 caliber weapons with the more effective .50 caliber gun and adopting the hydraulically operated, enclosed gun turrets pioneered by the British. Armor and self-sealing fuel tanks were also incorporated, and together with heavy ammunition loads, sharply reduced the weight of bombs each aircraft could deliver. ("We've got tons of ammunition, and a teeny bloody bomb," ran a sarcastic RAF lyric.) The bombers flew in tight formations so that the defensive fire from several aircraft could be brought to bear on any attacker.

Night bombing

After a few daylight raids were practically massacred by the Luftwaffe, Bomber Command withdrew to the cover of night. The bombers did not fly in formation, which would have been impossible at night, but in a long, wide stream. Crews who demonstrated good navigational skills were formed into special Pathfinder squadrons, which headed the stream and marked the target with flares. The Pathfinders were the first units to be equipped with electronic devices such as Gee (a receiver for radio beacons, which allowed a skilled navigator to fix his aircraft's position with much greater accuracy than earlier methods) and H2S (a radar which displayed a crude map of the ground below and ahead of the aircraft). Even with the help of the Pathfinders, however, there was no way to strike individual factories at night. Instead, the RAF sent bombers in massive numbers against industrial cities, hoping to cause widespread devastation with high-explosive and incendiary bombs.

The advantages of cover of night diminished as the war progressed. Night fighters were fitted with airborne radar, and other radar systems were developed to aim heavy anti-aircraft guns. The RAF retained its turreted .30 caliber defensive guns but did not greatly increase their number. In fact, the guns of a single bomber were of very little use against night fighters. The gunners served as lookouts; if a fighter was spotted in time, the pilot could throw his aircraft into a "corkscrew" maneuver, a series of climbs, dives and turns which the night fighter, with its crude radar, could not track.

EW

Where the RAF did improve its defenses was in the completely new realm of electronic warfare (EW). By 1944, most of the basic tools of EW had been invented: listening devices, by which the crew could tell that they were being detected; chaff, or clouds of aluminum foil which created strong false echoes on enemy radar screens; and jammers of various types, which sent out strong radio-frequency signals to obliterate the images on airborne and ground-based radar screens or to prevent pilots from hearing their ground controllers. Complex deception exercises, in which streams of obsolete bombers were sent in the general direction of a likely target to draw fighters to the wrong area, were carried out on many occasions.

Despite heavy guns and EW, the pattern of both the RAF and USAAF campaigns was one of heavy losses and occasional disasters. In October 1943, the 8th Air Force lost sixty out of 291 Fortresses in a raid on Schweinfurt; in March 1944, Bomber Command lost ninety-six out of 795 aircraft launched against Nuremberg. By the spring of 1944, when the strategic bombing campaign was suspended because of the need to prepare for the D-Day invasion, Bomber Command was suffering regular losses on a scale which would have made continued operations impossible; the odds were against any crew completing a first tour of operations. As for the USAAF, it was only the introduction

The North American P-51 Mustang, one of the first fighters that could escort bombers all the way to Berlin, arrived just as it became clear that defensive guns alone were no match for the Luftwaffe.

Boeing's B-29 was designed to carry a sophisticated system of low-drag turrets, remotely controlled by gunners in the fuse-lage. However, the bomber was successful only when the turrets were removed and targets were hit at night. Boeing

of new variants of the P-47 and P-51 fighters, with enough range to escort bombers to Berlin, which saved the 8th Air Force from defeat.

Despite the lessons from the European theater, the USAAF pressed ahead in the war years with a program of bomber development which evolved in a straight line from the Fortress and the Liberator, envisioning similar tactics even though there was no sign of any escort fighter which could match the range of future bombers. The program encompassed two generations of development and two main aircraft types. The first to start was Boeing's B-29; a $3.6 million contract for two prototypes was signed in August 1940. The B-29 was to be faster and higher-flying than the B-17 and B-24, with pressurized accommodation for its crew, and was to carry a defensive armament of ten .50 caliber guns in remotely-controlled turrets. At the same time, however, it was to have a much heavier bombload than the older bombers and a 2,000 mile radius of action. The performance was to be made possible by much more efficient aerodynamic and structural design and new turbosupercharged 2,200 horsepower engines.

Super-long-range bombers

In November 1941—before the United States was at war, and ten months before the XB-29 flew—the USAAF ordered two pairs of prototype bombers which carried the philosophy of a heavily armed, high-altitude daylight bomber another great step forward. Fearing the defeat of the United Kingdom, the USAAF had called for a bomber capable of flying 10,000 miles with a 10,000 pound bombload; neat round numbers which were roughly twice the targets for the B-29. Two designs were selected for development. Consolidated Aircraft's XB-36 was conventional except for its pusher engine installation and its awesome size. It measured 230 feet from wingtip to wingtip and would weigh about twice as much as the B-29, which itself would be one of the world's heaviest aircraft when it flew. It would defend itself from fighter attack with a battery of sixteen twenty-millimeter cannon housed in eight remotely-controlled turrets, six of which would retract into the fuselage to reduce drag in cruising flight. The rival to the XB-36 was only two thirds as heavy, but was designed to carry as many bombs just as far, by virtue of its radically different configuration: it was the Northrop XB-35, later known as the Flying Wing.

Britain did not fall, the B-29 had enough range to cross the seas around Japan, and development of the 10,000 mile bombers was rightly allowed to slip in favor of priority wartime programs. The fact remained, however, that the basic design of the two giants, like that of the B-29, was complete long before the Allied strategic bombing campaign against Germany started, and was fundamentally affected by prewar theories rather than the lessons of combat. The XB-36 and XB-35 prototypes were in final assembly as the bomber war in Europe and the Pacific entered its penultimate stage. Events in this stage were to be most important in the development of bomber doctrine and technology in the postwar years.

Mosquito

In 1942, Bomber Command had carried out the first of many daylight nuisance raids using a radical multi-purpose military aircraft, the de Havilland Mosquito. Developed by the small,

clubby de Havilland company despite minimal official interest, the Mosquito was adopted as a night fighter and reconnaissance aircraft first, and later as a bomber. At first, losses were high and the two-man crew could not handle the tasks of navigation and accurate bomb-aiming. Late in 1942, however, tests started with a new radio navigation aid called Oboe. Highly accurate, but limited in range by the curvature of the Earth, Oboe was very suited to the Mosquito, which could cruise at 28,000 feet or more with a bombload and could, therefore, bomb the industrial cities of the Ruhr under guidance from the Oboe ground stations in Britain.

Bomber Command consolidated its Mosquito day-bomber squadrons with its Oboe/Mosquito Pathfinder units in mid-1943, forming the Light Night Striking Force (LNSF) to perform diversionary attacks and to force the Luftwaffe to send up night-fighters when the main force was not flying. Developments proceeded rapidly. By 1944, Bomber Command was taking delivery of Mosquito B.XVI bombers with improved Merlin engines and pressurized cockpits, which could carry as many bombs as far as a B-17. Some of them carried the new H2S Mk VI bombing radar, but no production Mosquito carried so much as a single defensive gun.

Losses of the high-flying, agile Mosquitoes were a tiny fraction of losses among the main force of slow heavies. Bomber Command's 8 Group, comprising the Pathfinders and the LNSF, flew more than 27,000 Mosquito missions, from which 108 aircraft failed to return. This was less than a tenth of the loss rate among the main force, and represented a total loss of aircrew (killed and missing) that was about one third of the total loss on the single Nuremberg raid in March 1944. One factor behind the low loss rate is worthy of note: the Mosquito was built of spruce, birch plywood and balsa wood, and presented a weak flicker on contemporary radar screens compared with a conventional heavy bomber.

The nuclear bomb

The US Army Air Force also performed a few missions, late in the war, which deviated from their orthodox tactics. Early in 1945, the hard-driving Major General Curtis E. LeMay took over the 21st Bomber Command. The Command's B-29s were based in the Mariana Islands, which had been retaken at immense cost so that the new bombers would be able to launch a sustained daylight precision bombing offensive against Japan's armaments industry. Results, by the end of 1944, had been disappointing in the extreme. High operating altitudes reduced the bombers' payloads and contributed to engine troubles, and cloud cover frequently forced the B-29s to bomb by radar, which was insufficiently accurate to hit point targets.

Late in February 1945, LeMay ordered that the 300-plus B-29s in his command be stripped of their technically marvelous gun turrets and, on March 9, sent them to bomb the center

Bomber Command's de Havilland Mosquitos had the lowest loss rates of any World War II bomber, thanks to high speed, high altitude and to some extent low radar reflectivity, a result of the bomber's wooden sandwich construction. Jay Miller/Aerofax

Despite its size and complexity, the B-36 was produced in quantity because it was the only airplane which would carry the atomic weapons of the day over intercontinental distances. The biggest of them all was the *first operational H-bomb, the MK17; the giant B-36 could carry two of them. Even the B-36 leaped skyward when this 41,400 pound, 20 megaton monster left the bomb shackles.* USAF via Chuck Hansen

of Tokyo at night, from less than 8,000 feet. Because of the lower altitude and the deletion of the guns, each aircraft could carry its maximum 22,000 pound bombload; LeMay had them loaded with napalm. Instead of flying in formation, the B-29s were launched singly, and would bomb individually by radar. The destruction caused by the Tokyo raid and the others that followed it was immense, and losses were minimal.

On August 6 and August 15, 1945, USAF B-29s dropped nuclear weapons on Hiroshima and Nagasaki. The world was changed forever. The bomber mission was to change less than one might think, particularly in relation to the tactics and doctrine which had evolved late in the war years.

Aftermath

One of the immediate implications of the nuclear bomb was that direct defense against it would never be enough. Even if an air-defense system could guarantee to inflict Schweinfurt-scale losses on an attacking force, hundreds of cities could be destroyed. The alternative was the doctrine of deterrence: nuclear attack would be prevented by the fear of an equally devastating counterattack. Bombers were the only means of delivering such an attack; in contrast to the disarmament and halt in weapons development that followed the 1914-18 war, the period after 1945 saw a surge in the development of bomber aircraft and of defensive systems to blunt bomber attacks.

Nuclear weapons also ended the controversy over the merits of daylight visual precision bombing versus nocturnal area bombing. Pinpoint accuracy was no longer relevant when a single bomb would devastate an entire city; radar would do the job in any weather.

Formation tactics were also rendered obsolete, because nuclear bombs were as scarce and expensive as they were powerful. No longer would hundreds of bombers be sent to one target; two aircraft would be the maximum. While tactics and ingress routes could be coordinated to heighten the stress on the defenses, each crew would essentially be on its own from the moment it entered hostile territory. There would be no way for another aircraft to mark the target, as Bomber Command's Pathfinders had done; each crew would be fully responsible for finding its own targets, and navigation would be as critical as ever.

The nuclear-armed bomber force could tolerate higher losses than wartime Bomber Command or the 8th, for the simple reason that there would be only one operation. However, survivability was still important, because it would be impossible to prepare a realistic targeting plan if many bombers failed to reach their objectives.

The new generation

The USAAF and the RAF—the only Western air forces with any hope of acquiring nuclear weapons in the foreseeable future—once again took separate approaches to survivability. The US Strategic Air Command (SAC) was formed in March 1946 with the world's only nuclear bombs and the only aircraft—the B-29—which was capable of delivering them without being immolated in the subsequent fireball. Five months later, in August, the first Convair XB-36 flew from Fort Worth, Texas. Even though it was basically designed as a daylight precision bomber, the immense B-36 was one of two aircraft under development which had enough range to reach the Soviet Union—no longer an ally but the United States' most likely adversary—from US bases. (The smaller Northrop XB-35 Flying Wing had flown in June 1946, but was being plagued with engine problems; already, it was considered more likely to be developed as a jet.) Between 1946 and 1949, the USAAF (reformed as the US Air Force in July 1947) fought tooth and nail for the B-36, despite many technical problems and the opposition of the US Navy, which wanted to deliver nuclear strikes from massive aircraft carriers.

B-36

It was mid-1950 before the B-36 became operational. It was never used in action, and most fighter pilots of the day would have argued that it was a sitting duck, capable of cruising at little more than 200 mph. At that time, however, the Soviet Union had no radar-equipped night fighters, so the only threat to the bombers would have been ground-controlled intercepts by single-seat day fighters such as MiG-15s. Much more advanced bombers, designed for the nuclear era, were under development to replace it long before it joined the squadrons.

SAC in its formative years was closely identified with General LeMay, who became its commander in October 1948.

This Convair B-36 may not seem to carry many defensive guns; in fact, no fewer than six remotely controlled turrets, each mounting a pair of 20 mm cannon, are hidden inside the fuselage. Originally designed with six piston engines, the B-36 was later fitted with four booster jets to give it a chance of survival against jet fighters. General Dynamics

Fast and technically radical, the Boeing B-47 represented as large an advance over its piston-engined predecessors as the B-2 does today.

Rather than the cigar-chomping, bomb-happy monster of legend, LeMay was an innovative commander whose most usual criticism was: "You can do better than that." (Its effect was often devastating.) He was also relentless in his war on slackness in any form, with a keen sense of when to fire a subordinate in order to bring others into line.

Almost every unit in LeMay's experience had failed in its first mission; but for SAC, there would only be one mission, and it had to be performed cor-rectly. Under LeMay, SAC was transformed into an organization on a war footing. Its approach was summed up by a senior officer in 1988: "In Strategic Air Command, we work very hard to define the best way to do something; then, we all do it that way all the time." A standard joke is that if you open any desk in SAC you will always find all the pencils in the same order.

B-47

LeMay bypassed the first generation of jet bombers developed by the US

The relatively short range of jet bombers cast doubts on their operational usefulness until Boeing and SAC developed the Flying Boom refueling technique. The operator "flies" a rigid, telescopic pipe into a slipway on the receiver aircraft. The Flying Boom can deliver fuel at a much greater rate than most flexible hose systems. Boeing

Britain's first jet bomber was the English Electric Canberra. Small, unarmed and capable of flying higher than most contemporary fighters, it was very much a "jet Mosquito" in its philosophy. Jay Miller/ Aerofax

industry in favor of the radical Boeing B-47. Representing a massive advance in structures, aerodynamics and flight control systems over previous bombers, the B-47 could cruise close to the maximum speed of contemporary fighters. Like the B-29s which LeMay had sent over Tokyo, it carried only tail guns for defense. It had no visual bombsight, but delivered

weapons by radar. The B-47's main drawback was its range, which was not great enough to reach deep inside the Soviet Union; however, Boeing and the USAF developed a new technique for midair refueling, using a rigid telescoping boom, fitted with small control fins so that an operator aboard the tanker aircraft could "fly" it into a socket on the bomber's nose. B-47s were also based in Britain, from where they could threaten many Soviet targets. The B-47 and its companion tanker, the Boeing KC-97, entered service in 1951.

While the B-47 was still an untested and controversial prototype, in early 1947, the RAF had issued its requirements for the first British nuclear bomber. Strongly reflecting Bomber Command's experience with the Mosquito, they represented a step beyond the B-47, as much in operational doctrine as in technology and performance. Specification B.35/46 called for a bomber capable of operating and maneuvering at (by the standards of the day) extreme alti-

High performance at high altitude was the aim of Britain's nuclear bombers, such as the Handley Page Victor. They could operate *well above 50,000 feet, considerably higher than the B-47.* Jay Miller/Aerofax

tudes, in excess of 50,000 feet. The idea was to present as difficult a target as possible to a small-winged fighter, which would be out of its element in the thin high-altitude air. The new bomber would carry a single nuclear weapon, and no guns; radar would be the prime means of weapon delivery, and electronic warfare systems were to be given high priority.

Valiant, Vulcan and Victor

The RAF finally acquired three new bombers. The Vickers Valiant was regarded as a low-risk design, available as a back-up in case of problems with the more advanced Avro Vulcan and Handley Page Victor. The Victor had a compound-sweep, crescent wing and T-tail, while the Vulcan was virtually a flying

Oddly reminiscent of the B-2, with its blended, geometrically simple shape, the Avro Vulcan was designed for high speed at high altitude. It could cruise above 60,000 feet and was largely immune from interception until SAMs proliferated in the early sixties. Jay Miller/Aerofax

A pristine B-52E, probably on an acceptance test flight from Boeing's Wichita, Kansas, plant. Efficient engines and advanced design gave the B-52 a remarkable range for a jet aircraft. Boeing

wing, with only a small vestige of a front fuselage breaking up its triangular shape. The Mark 1 versions of the Vulcan and Victor could operate routinely at altitudes well above 50,000 feet, and the improved B.2 models could fly above 60,000 feet with a normal bombload.

B-52

Aviation technology surged ahead in the fifties, with LeMay's SAC firmly in the vanguard, confident that they could handle and operate any conceivable system, with enough training and the right leadership. While the Vulcan and Victor were to be the last British strategic bombers, the USAF ordered prototypes of a faster replacement for the lumbering B-36 from Boeing in July 1948. The new XB-52 was to be powered by turboprops—gas turbines geared to propellers. Three months later, however, the original design was thrown out in favor of a faster, pure jet design, thanks to the success of the B-47 and the development of more efficient jet engines; the definitive configuration was outlined by a handful of Boeing engineers in an epic weekend at a Dayton, Ohio, hotel, halfway through a series of presentations to the USAF at neighboring Wright-Patterson Air Force Base.

This new bomber made its first flight on April 15, 1952. Seven days later, Boeing decided to put its own money into developing the so-called Model 367-80: a transport, using similar aerodynamic and propulsion technology, which would also serve as an improved tanker to match the B-52's range and fuel capacity.

Boeing ended the B-52 line with the B-52H. Externally very similar to the B-52E, the B-52H was a radically different aircraft with much more internal fuel capacity (note that the underwing tanks are much smaller), more efficient engines and underwing pylons, here occupied by Skybolt ballistic missiles.

At the time of publication, four decades after that weekend in Dayton, the B-52 is still the USAF's most important strategic bomber and it is still refueled routinely by KC-135 tankers developed from the Model 367-80. The story of the modern bomber is the story of how this situation, totally different from any plans and expectations in 1952, came about.

SAC and the ICBM

In the early fifties, the bomber was threatened from many directions. The USAF's Air Defense Command was preparing to receive supersonic, all-weather, missile-armed interceptors and it was only a matter of time before their opposite numbers in PVO-Strany, the Soviet Union's Air Defense Troops of the Homeland, were similarly equipped.

Surface-to-air guided missiles, first developed by German engineers in the last years of the war, were reaching the point of being acceptable for service use. Early-warning radars were being improved. Above all, massive computers were being developed which could track radar targets automatically, work out their speeds and headings, and steer an interceptor or long-range missile toward the best interception point.

Some people already argued that the day of the manned bomber was passing. As long ago as 1946, the USAAF had issued a contract to Northrop to develop a subsonic intercontinental cruise missile, later known as the SM-62 Snark. It was followed by the Mach 3 North American SM-64 Navaho. However, both these programs were overshadowed, overhauled and eventually superseded by

Boeing used their own money to develop a jet tanker, specifically to refuel the B-52. It was ordered by the USAF as the KC-135. No replacement is in sight, and the KC-135 will remain in service well into the next century. Some will undoubtedly see 50 years of active use. Boeing

The USAF readily embraced the missile age. Northrop's 30 ton SM-62 Snark cruise missile was the first unmanned intercontinental weapon to enter development, but it was *withdrawn from service only months after it was declared operational in 1961. Its astro-inertial guidance system was adapted for the Lockheed A-12 and SR-71. Northrop*

Even more radical than the Snark, the North American XSM-64 Navaho missile was designed to have intercontinental range at Mach 3. It, too, was scrapped in favor of ICBMs.

the intercontinental ballistic missile (ICBM).

Most parts of the ICBM program presented enormous challenges of their own: its massive rocket motors; the technology to guide it to its target; and the new materials which would ensure that its warhead (re-entry vehicle, or RV) did not burn up as it fell back into the atmosphere. Engineers gradually solved the problems, however; the cancellation of the Navaho, in 1957, was precipitated by the solution of the last major problems of the Convair SM-65 Atlas, the first operational US ICBM. The control of all US long-range rockets was assigned to SAC in November 1956.

Missiles were faster than aircraft and their toughened re-entry vehicles were hard to destroy, while aircraft seemed increasingly vulnerable. Moreover, missiles needed no training flights. Their crews ran through firing drills, but the missiles stayed on the ground, using no fuel and requiring only enough maintenance to keep them ready to fly.

B-52 development

As the development of the ICBM continued, SAC worked to maintain the survivability of its manned bombers, under increasing pressure to justify their cost and effectiveness. The early B-52 models were followed by the B-52G, which entered service in 1959 and became the most widely produced B-52 subtype. Internally, the B-52G was almost a new design, with much greater fuel capacity, a refined airframe and improved electronics. The extra fuel allowed the B-52G to follow more tortuous, less predictable tracks toward its targets. It could also carry a pair of North American GAM-77 (later, AGM-28) Hound Dog missiles under its wings. These were small supersonic cruise missiles, carrying a warhead in the megaton class, designed to destroy or disable missile sites in the bomber's path. Inside its bomb bay, the B-52G could also carry McDonnell GAM-72 (later, ADM-20) Quail decoy missiles. With the aid of radar reflectors inside its fiberglass airframe, the Quail appeared on radar

The B-52H was developed as a long-endurance carrier for GAM-87 Skybolt air-launched ballistic missiles, but became a penetrating bomber when the missile was scrapped in 1962. The four Skybolts represent a 20 ton external load. Smithsonian Institution

SAC combined the missile and the bomber with the development of the Hound Dog supersonic cruise missile, designed to attack *fighter bases in the bomber's path.* Jay Miller/Aerofax

screens to be as large as a B-52; it also carried transmitters which imitated a B-52's electronic jamming systems. Each B-52G carried two Quails, tripling the number of targets for the defenses to engage. All this gear could be carried because nuclear and thermonuclear bombs had shrunk, since the early fif-

ties, to a small fraction of their original size and weight.

B-58

While the B-52G joined the squadrons, the next generation was already under development. Convair had been authorized to proceed with the first supersonic bomber, the B-58, in early

Faced by the threat of supersonic fighters, SAC developed a high-altitude, Mach 2 strategic bomber, the General Dynamics B-58. In order to attain a minimal strategic range, its designers equipped the B-58 with a mas-
sive centerline pod which contained a nuclear bomb and much of the airplane's fuel. The entire pod was to be dropped on the target, leaving a light, small, low-drag airplane for the return flight. General Dynamics

1953; prototypes were ordered in the following year, and the first XB-58 flew in November 1956. A radical and complex aircraft, stuffed with extremely advanced electronic warfare and navigation equipment, the B-58 was designed to attack heavily defended targets with a single multi-megaton thermonuclear weapon, making its bomb run at 55,000 feet and Mach 2 to evade the defenses. The weapon and much of the B-58's fuel were housed in an enormous ventral pod.

XB-70 Valkyrie

Even the B-58 looked modest beside what SAC wanted in a replacement for the B-52. The basic operational requirement, issued in October 1954, called for a 7,000 mile range, a 50,000 pound payload and as high a speed over the target as possible. It was understood that SAC wanted Mach 2 or more.

The requirement was so demanding that in February 1955, the USAF issued two specifications: Weapon System 110A (WS-110A) for a bomber fueled by kerosene or other chemical fuel, and WS-125A for a nuclear-powered bomber. Nuclear aircraft propulsion had been under development since 1951, and the idea was that WS-125A would loiter for days outside enemy territory on nuclear power, and use turbojets or ramjets for its final dash on the target.

Boeing and North American responded to WS-110A with designs which

The Pentagon spent over $500 million in the fifties on the development of nuclear power for aircraft. The General Dynamics NX-2, shown here, was proposed as a test-bed for a nuclear jet engine, in the center-section. The conventional jet engines under the wings would have been needed for take-off and climb. General Dynamics

carried the B-58 concept one step further. Instead of a single mission pod, the WS-110A designs both featured two vast auxiliary fuel tanks attached to jettisonable outboard wing sections. The "floating" outer wings were flexibly attached to the basic airframe, and carried their own weight and that of the fuel tanks. The complete wing was much lighter than a one-piece wing of the same span.

Both proposals were rejected in March 1957, after new aerodynamic studies indicated that an aircraft could be designed to cruise at Mach 3 throughout its flight, meet the SAC payload-range requirement and still be lighter than the subsonic-cruise designs. The secret lay in aerodynamic work which suggested that an aircraft could be shaped to recover some of its supersonic wave drag in the form of lift. An additional improvement in performance was promised through the use of fuels containing a slurry of boron, which would yield more energy per pound than kerosene. Both Boeing and North American re-submitted their WS-110A proposals, and the latter's design was announced as the contest winner in December 1957.

The high performance promised by the XB-70, as the new bomber was designated, contrasted with the lackluster figures being generated by WS-125A studies. Calculations of thrust, reactor weight and shielding weight continued to show that a nuclear-powered aircraft would have trouble dragging its own weight off the ground, let alone the fuel needed for a supersonic dash. WS-125A was canceled in early 1958, although the remnants of the airborne nuclear power program lingered into 1961.

The XB-70, named Valkyrie, was the most expensive and visible aircraft program of its day, as the B-29, and B-36 and B-52 had been before it. It was the heaviest aircraft in the world and—with the exception of the Central Intelligence Agency's secret Lockheed A-12—it was also the fastest. Many of its features, such as its stainless-steel honeycomb construction and its enormous moving wingtips, were completely new. Intended as a fully operational bomber, it naturally required a complete new generation of navigation, attack and defensive systems.

ALBM

By the end of the fifties, however, the Pentagon was spending billions on nuclear missiles such as land-based ICBMs and the Navy's submarine-launched Polaris. And SAC was developing a third new class of weapon: the Douglas GAM-87 Skybolt air-launched ballistic missile (ALBM). A primary attack weapon, rather than a defense-suppression system like Hound Dog, Skybolt combined a megaton-class warhead and a stellar-inertial navigation system in a thirty-eight foot, 11,300 pound, 1,000 mile range missile. The new B-52H was developed specifically to carry four Skybolts on wing pylons.

To justify this range of weapons, SAC argued that their capabilities and vulnerabilities complemented one another. ICBMs were invulnerable to interception, but their accuracy was still poor and their warheads were only a small fraction of a heavy bomber's payload. They were more effective against large, soft targets such as cities than they were against military objectives, which could be sheltered against blast and radiation. Missiles could not be recalled after launch, so they would only be launched once a full-scale attack was in progress. SAC reasoned that such an attack would destroy many ICBMs on the ground. The argument may have been sound in theory but was overriden by financial necessity.

Survivability

Of all the new weapons, high-altitude, high-speed bombers appeared to be the most readily countered by an adversary, through the development and production of faster fighters and bigger, longer-range surface-to-air missiles (SAMs). The latter were a more serious threat in the long term, for the same economic reasons that favored the ICBM over the bomber. SAMs did not require highly skilled pilots and did not burn fuel on training flights, and the electronics (which accounted for much of the cost of any system's maintenance over its lifetime) functioned in a relatively benign ground environment.

Return to low-level tactics

On May 1, 1960, a barrage of Soviet SA-2 missiles knocked a CIA U-2 spyplane out of the sky near Sverdlovsk. The U-2 had been designed to fly at altitudes which no Soviet fighter or missile could reach. It had done so with impunity for four years, but the 1960 incident made it hard to argue the case for any high-altitude aircraft.

But the bomber proved, once again, equal to the challenge. Any system reliant on ground-based radars has an Achilles heel. The radar cannot see beyond the horizon, and its range against low-flying targets is thereby limited. Some special missions had been flown "under the radar" in the 1939-45 war; they were risky, mainly because the bombers were vulnerable to light flak over the immediate target area. However, nuclear weapons and jet speeds provided a number of options to deal with that problem. The bomber could enter a short, steep climb just before reaching the target and "toss" the bomb

Supersonic interceptors such as the General Dynamics F-106 presented a major threat to the manned bomber. Powerful ground-based *computers would guide the aircraft into position for an attack with guided missiles.* General Dynamics

onto the objective, performing a half-loop, a half-roll and dive to escape. Radar-aimed flak could be jammed, or a "stand-off bomb" with a small rocket motor could be fired from just outside SAM range.

Technology was alleviating other problems associated with low-level tactics. Aircraft, particularly jets, consume so much more fuel per mile at low altitude that in 1950 it was hard to envisage a bomber capable of penetrating to inland Soviet targets below the radar fence. But the "wet-wing" B-52G had a range superior to that of the B-52D, while the B-52H with its turbofan engines was considerably better yet. The new, smaller nuclear weapons allowed the bombers to carry more fuel. KC-135 jet tankers were available in large numbers. Electronic intelligence and reconnaissance made it possible to plan routes in which the bombers would drop to low altitude only when necessary, exploiting gaps in the defenses. Doppler and iner-

tial navigation systems helped bomber crews follow these routes accurately without the aid of long-range radar maps.

The conversion to low-level operations in SAC took place between 1960 and 1965. The implications for future bomber development were enormous. The air at low altitudes is so dense, relative to the air at normal cruising heights, that it is virtually impossible for a manned aircraft to sustain speeds much greater than 900 mph, or Mach 1.2. Even this requires tremendous power, and subsonic flight at 650 mph or Mach 0.9 is more efficient. At such speeds, an aircraft such as the B-58, designed for Mach 2 cruise, is operating far below its design maximum speed, and is both over-designed and inefficient. The B-70 would be even worse off. At low altitude, the B-52 would easily outperform either supersonic aircraft.

The outcome was predictable. B-58 production stopped after 116 aircraft

Early Soviet air defense fighters operated under very close ground control over a limited range. As a result, the fighters such as the MiG-21 were small and relatively cheap, and could be built in large numbers.

had been built, and the type equipped only two SAC wings. Production of the B-70 was canceled in 1959, reinstated in 1960 and finally canceled in 1961. Two prototypes of the B-70 were built, but long before the first of them flew, in December 1964, the aircraft had been relegated to research. Skybolt was scrapped, too, in November 1962, because it promised to be extremely expensive while doing nothing that could not be done better by Polaris or land-based missiles.

This left the B-52, which proved remarkably adaptable to low-level operations, once some structural strengthening had been carried out. It has not suffered major structural problems since. This is not to say that the B-52 is immune from the effects of age, but that it has not required repairs that were unjustifiably expensive. In its thirty-plus years of service, it has been modified to carry weapons which were not imaginable when it was designed. What cannot be accommodated in its cavernous weapon bay can be hung under the inner wings, on the stations originally designed for Hound Dogs and Skybolts. It may look ungainly from some angles, with its slab-sided body, angular wings and its unique quadricycle landing gear, but it is an extremely efficient aircraft, almost perfectly matched to any mission which involves hauling bombs and missiles over long distances at high subsonic speeds.

The strongest testimonial for the B-52 is that it has taken so long to produce a replacement which seems to be worth the money. The design of that aircraft started as soon as Defense Secretary McNamara drove the last nail into the B-70's coffin in January 1962, publicly stating that the Kennedy administration was opposed to its development as a weapon. At that point, the bomber's advocates realized that it would be at least mid-1965 before a hypothetical new administration could reverse the decision, and by that time it would be too late.

Birth of the B-1A

The next bomber, the USAF decided, would need to have better performance

Designed to a requirement which was almost beyond the state of the art, the B-58 was a "hot," unforgiving airplane and was expensive to maintain. Its safety record was poor, and the decision to retire the force was taken only three years after the last B-58 was delivered. General Dynamics

at low altitude, flying faster and lower than the B-52 could fly, hugging the contours of the ground more tightly to present a more difficult target for fighters. It would have a longer range at low altitude, so that it could use terrain cover over longer segments of its flight and follow less direct, less predictable routes to its targets deep within the Soviet Union. However, SAC still wanted the new bomber to be supersonic at high altitude, if only to force the Soviet defenses to keep their expensive long-range missiles and high-altitude fighters in service.

F-111

The technology to produce such a bomber was within reach. In 1961, the USAF had started development of the General Dynamics F-111, a new tactical bomber which combined variable sweep-back or "swing wings" with augmented turbofan engines. The new aircraft promised to be remarkably versatile. For take-off, the wings were spread wide; the engines, at full augmented thrust, produced an unprecedented amount of power for their weight, and the aircraft could lift a massive load of fuel and bombs into the air. Once in the air, the augmentors were cut and the engines changed from roaring, fuel-thirsty Mr. Hydes into thrifty Dr. Jekylls; with its long, efficient wing, the aircraft had much better range than a conventional supersonic fighter.

Over hostile territory, the F-111 could sweep its wings back and drop below the radar horizon, where it could fly at more than 600 mph for hundreds of miles, a few hundred feet off the ground, thanks to the low drag and

Last of the supersonic, high-level bombers was the 2,000 mph North American XB-70. Production plans were dropped before the XB-70 flew, and the two prototypes were used for research.

Defense Secretary Robert McNamara, an enemy of the manned bomber, wanted to replace most SAC bombers with the General Dynamics FB-111A, adapted from Tactical Air Command's F-111E. Armed with SRAM missiles, and operated at their maximum overload weights from the northeastern United States, the FB-111As are still assigned to targets on the periphery of the Soviet Union. General Dynamics

superior ride quality provided by its short, highly swept wing. Terrain-following radar (in fact, a terrain-detection radar coupled to a multiplex automatic control system) enabled the aircraft to use this performance at night or in cloud. Lastly, with wings swept back and the augmentors lit, the F-111 could hit Mach 2.5 at altitude—if only for a few minutes.

AMSA

By 1965, SAC's desired new strategic bomber was taking the form of a grown-up F-111, with a swing-wing and augmented turbofan engines. However, it would be three to four times bigger, to give it the necessary range and payload. Boeing, General Dynamics and North American Rockwell were issued contracts to produce preliminary designs. Because "bomber" was still an explosive word on Capitol Hill and in the Office of the Secretary of Defense, the study was labeled as the Advanced Manned Strategic Aircraft (AMSA).

AMSA was to remain a study and nothing more as long as Robert McNamara had anything to do with it, and in the last three years of the Johnson administration the acronym was sometimes said to stand for "America's Most Studied Aircraft." Meanwhile, in December 1965, McNamara set a timetable for the retirement of all the SAC bombers which did not have a significant low-level penetration capability; the B-58 and all the B-52s except the G and H models would be retired by June 1971. (The last of the $30 million B-58s had been delivered barely three years before McNamara's announcement; it was the least desirable of the type's many world records.)

Two days after this decision fell on the SAC bomber community, McNamara announced a consolation prize: SAC would receive 263 FB-111As, slightly modified versions of the tactical F-111E. The FB-111A would have short legs for a bomber, and would be dependent on aerial refueling to reach even the periphery of the Soviet Union, but its low-level penetration capability, accurate navigation system and ability to carry the new Short-Range Attack Missile (SRAM) under development by Boeing counted in its favor. Politics played a part, as well: the F-111 program, the epitome of McNamara's philosophy, was in deep technical trouble, and adding another 263 aircraft to the production run would make the aircraft look more successful. It was also a Texan product under a Texas administration.

Flight-testing of the FB-111A was well under way in November 1968, when Richard Nixon (a California Republican) was elected president. His new Secretary of Defense, Melvin Laird, wasted no time in reversing McNamara's course. In March 1969, Laird announced that FB-111A production was to be stopped after seventy-four aircraft—four squadrons and spares—had been completed, and that more money would be provided in 1969 and 1970 for AMSA.

Rockwell design selected

In November 1969, the USAF issued a request for proposals (RFP) for a new bomber. The RFP invited manufacturers to submit AMSA designs to the USAF's Aeronautical Systems Division, together with their proposed plans and estimated costs for detail design and the construction and testing of prototypes. As usual, the industry was given ninety days to respond. Six months later, the USAF selected Rockwell International, formerly North American, to develop the new bomber. Because one of McNamara's actions had been to impose a single new system of aircraft designations on the US services, and this was the first bomber to be ordered since the new system took effect, it became the B-1A.

The Rockwell B-1A would be a swing-wing airplane, almost as heavy as a B-52, would carry a crew of four and be fitted with comprehensive electronic jamming equipment. It would fly at Mach 2 at high altitude, or at 600 mph close to the ground. It would match the older bomber's range and carry a heavier payload. It would also be designed so that it could leave its bases as quickly as possible in the event of an attack, and survive the detonation of nuclear weapons in its immediate vicinity.

The USAF planned to build 240 B-1s, the first of them entering service late in the seventies. The aircraft itself was so complex that it would take more than four years before the first prototype flew, and it would be six years at least before the fourth prototype would start testing the vital electronic equipment.

While carpenters and welders in Rockwell's El Segundo, California, factory started to assemble an imposing full-size mock-up of the new bomber, some fundamental changes in aerospace technology were threatening the project with built-in obsolescence. Some of these changes were already reflected in a number of development programs, none of them very large and many of them highly secret. In small teams and small companies, aircraft engineers, electrical engineers, computer specialists, operations analysts and materials specialists were developing a radical approach to military aircraft design. It was so new that in 1970 it barely had a name, but it soon became known as Stealth.

Vanishing tricks

"One-two-three! And where's your breakfast?" Leopard stared, and
Ethiopian stared, but all they could see were stripy shadows and blotchy
shadows in the forest, but never a sign of Zebra and Giraffe.

Rudyard Kipling, "Just So Stories"

In a corner of a dusty hangar, in a Washington suburb, rests the prototype of the first Stealth bomber, a flying wing which, in its production form, was to have been built from radar-absorbing materials. Conceived only five years after the first air-defense radars entered service, it never got beyond the flight-test stage. Had it done so, it might have bombed London or spied on the D-Day invasion ports, because it was built by a group known as *Sonderkommando 9* (Special Commando 9) for Hitler's Luftwaffe.

That the story of the Horten HoIX is so obscure is a clue to the real question behind Stealth, which is not so much "why now?" as "why not earlier?" There are good answers for both questions in the history of Stealth which, in fact, was some thirty years old before the HoIX was designed.

In the early summer of 1912, a resident of the Vienna suburbs might have glanced up at the still novel sound of an airplane overhead, only to see something strange, a skeletal airplane consisting of little more than sticks, wires and an engine. Hauptmann Petrocz von Petroczy was testing his new idea, an airplane that would survive its reconnaissance flights over enemy lines by virtue of being invisible.

It was basically a standard Etrich Taube monoplane, but Petroczy had had it covered with Emaillit, a transparent celluloid material produced by a company in Paris. Over the succeeding four years, similar experiments were carried out in Germany, using a similar synthetic material called Cellon. Perhaps a dozen aircraft were tested with Cellon covering, ranging from Fokker E III monoplane fighters to two massive biplane bombers.

Unfortunately, it was found that the Cellon covering, which was applied wet and contracted to a taut, smooth surface as it dried, tended to undergo a reverse process on contact with moisture, becoming dangerously slack during long periods of wet weather. Neither was there any firm evidence that the transparent covering would be of any use in combat. It seemed to become more opaque under cloudy conditions, and it was not transparent when viewed at an angle. The Imperial German Inspectorate of Aviation Troops issued a brief, largely negative report; the project was stopped so effectively that seventy years passed before any detailed account of it was published.

There are three lessons from the story of the invisible Fokkers. One is that there is usually a price to be paid for making an aircraft less visible. The second lesson is that it is not enough to make the aircraft less detectable; its

detectability, or "observability" must be reduced enough to make a difference in the real world. The third lesson is that the idea of making a combat aircraft more survivable by making it less detectable is as old as aviation. However, history had been so thoroughly forgotten that it seemed like the newest idea in the world when the word "Stealth" was introduced into public discussion in the summer of 1980.

Simply put, the purpose of Stealth or low-observables (LO) is to improve the ability of a weapon system to carry out its mission, by making it more difficult to detect. Stealth is intended to delay detection and to make it harder to track the target's course after detection. In the case of a true Stealth aircraft, the goal is to achieve such a high level of Stealth that the system will probably

Cellon transparent covering was applied to the rear fuselage and tail of the Linke-Hoffman R I 8/15, one of Imperial Germany's little-known Riesenflugzeug *(giant aircraft) class of the super-heavy bombers.*

The four engines were mounted internally, driving the propellers through extension shafts, so that they could be tended in flight. Peter M. Grosz collection

perform its mission without being detected at all.

The important word here is probably. There is no such thing as an invisible aircraft. But neither is there certainty in a military operation. If the probability of detection is reduced, the chances that the vehicle will survive and complete its mission are accordingly increased.

Reducing detectability

Stealth can be a consideration in the design of other weapons. Ship and tank designs can benefit from an analysis of why they are detectable, and what can be done to reduce the risks of detection. In fact, one entire branch of military science has been dominated by Stealth since its inception: submarine warfare. Avoiding detection, mainly by reducing submerged noise, but partly through designing sonar-resistant hulls and using anechoic (anti-echo) coatings, has been, and remains, one of the main thrusts of submarine design.

For submarine warfare, this was a natural development, since the main reason for building a submersible warship in the first place was to avoid detection. Air warfare was different. Flight performance—speed, range and maneuverability—and firepower were considered to be the most important attributes of the military aircraft, from the first air combats over France in World War I to the Vietnam era.

Visual detection

It was obvious that detectability was a factor in air combat. The pilot who sees his opponent first has time to maneuver into an advantageous position (between his opponent and the sun, for instance) and has the advantage of

surprise. The problem, in the early years of military aviation, was that there was not much to be done to reduce detectability. Up to the late thirties, the only target acquisition and identification device in service was the unaided human eye. The eye is limited in range, but its resolution (ability to distinguish detail) is extremely high, and it is difficult to fool. The only way to delay optical detection, it seemed, was to make the target smaller in linear dimensions (what the eye sees). But dimensions do not vary directly with weight, so a very large reduction in the weight of the aircraft would be needed to make any significant impact on visibility. While small size and lower detectability were touted as an advantage of some lightweight fighters of the thirties, their disadvantages—fewer guns, less armor, less range—were more glaringly obvious and few were built.

Electronic detection

Caught up in the race between the means of air attack and the means of defense described in the previous chapter, most engineers, planners and airmen missed the full significance of the changes in the nature of air combat in the forties and fifties. While air defense had been greatly reinforced by radar, it was also becoming dependent on it, for two reasons. One was that electronic aids developed in parallel with radar and, later, radar itself made it possible for the bomber to strike accurately at night or in bad weather; the other reason was that speeds and altitudes had outrun the capability of the human eye. With a supersonic interceptor and a high-subsonic bomber running toward each other at closing speeds approaching 2,000 mph, the fighter pilot would see his target far too late to start an interception. The bomber would be gone before he could turn to chase it.

Only a handful of people understood that it was no longer necessary for a bomber or other aircraft to be invisible, or small to the eye, in order for it to be so much less detectable that its ability to survive would be usefully increased. Radar engineers soon realized that the reflectivity of a radar target was not necessarily proportional to its size, adopting a measure of reflectivity called "radar cross section" (RCS) in order to provide a standard against which the performance of different radars could be compared. Sir Robert Watson-Watt, the pioneer of British radar, noted as early as 1935 that it would be logical for future heavy bombers to be designed so as to reduce their radar reflectivity.

RAM

During the 1939-45 war, the United States and Britain pursued aggressive and successful radar programs. By the war's end, radar systems were being produced or developed for fighter aircraft of all sizes, for bombers, to warn of fighter attack or to identify targets, and for anti-shipping aircraft. Perhaps as a response to this activity, German scientists led the way in developing materials which would absorb radar waves, rather than reflecting them (radar-absorbent material, or RAM). Two early types of RAM were employed operationally to shield the large snorkel tubes of later U-boats from detection by Allied ASV (air-to-surface-vessel) radar, under the codename *Schornfeinsteger* (chimney-sweep).

Neither were aircraft ignored. In the last months of the war, the brothers

Rear view of the Horten HoIX V2 under construction in November 1944. The HoIX V2 was the only powered HoIX to fly, and was destroyed during tests. Note the rearward extension of the trailing edge, a feature pioneered by the Horten brothers and emulated on the B-2. H. Weishaupt Verlag

Walter and Reimar Horten and a small team of workers tested the prototype of a radical flying-wing combat aircraft, the HoIX. The prototype had solid plywood wing skins, but the production version was to have been skinned with a sandwich material comprising two thin plywood sheets and a core made of sawdust, charcoal and glue. The material was expressly intended to absorb radar waves, and the Hortens realized that the reflective steel engines (buried in the center section) and steel-tube substructure of the aircraft would be concealed under the absorbent skin.

It is questionable whether the material would have been effective, even against the less sophisticated radars of the day. As will be seen later, the design of RAM is a complex matter. But such questions paled beside what the Horten brothers had accomplished. Their design was to achieve lower detectability by a combination of a suitable external shape and integral RAM, built into the load-bearing structure. It was almost two decades before it was more generally realized that this was the best, indeed virtually the only, way to build a less detectable aircraft which could accomplish a useful mission.

Like other German aircraft designers, the Horten brothers were not accorded the red-carpet treatment given to Germany's rocket scientists. Their work was clumsily picked over; Reimar Horten's offers of help for British and American flying-wing designers were rebuffed, and after the development and construction of aircraft in Germany was banned indefinitely, in 1947, Reimar Horten took his knowledge to Argentina. The third prototype of the HoIX, which had been completed but never flown, was taken to Wright-Patterson AFB for analysis. (It was then handed over to the Smithsonian Institution, and, in late 1988, was still stored at the National Air and Space Museum's facility in Silver Hill, Maryland.)

Meanwhile, American and British research into RAM began to achieve results. In the United States, a team at the Massachusetts Institute of Technology (MIT) Radiation Laboratory worked between 1941 and 1945, finally producing two materials known as Halpern anti-radar paint (HARP). One version of HARP consisted of iron particles embedded in a thick layer of neoprene rubber, and was intended for shipboard use. The other, developed under the USAAF designation MX-410, consisted of tiny disc-shaped aluminum flakes in a rubber matrix, and proved extremely effective even when applied in a thin layer.

These early forms of RAM were used in quite considerable quantities, but hardly at all on aircraft except in a few classified test programs. In Britain, the Royal Navy and the Plessey company developed absorbent materials to prevent the metal masts and superstructures of warships from interfering with their search and fire-control radars, while US companies such as Goodyear and BF Goodrich developed absorbers for radar test chambers.

There were two basic reasons for the slow application of this technology to aircraft. The first was that the "user community" (the pilots and former pilots who most strongly influence what aircraft projects are funded) was committed in the fifties and sixties to the development of bigger, faster warplanes with ever more sophisticated electronic systems. The idea of reducing detectability meant slowing, stopping or even reversing that trend, and the price in terms of the missiles, radars and other gadgets which would have to be abandoned in the process seemed too high.

The second reason for the limited use of RAM on aircraft was that it did not seem to do enough to justify its weight and cost. Even the best RAM, applied to a normal aircraft, will usually generate mediocre results. The lesson of the Horten HoIX design—that the way to slash RCS is to consider both electromagnetics and aerodynamics in the design of an aircraft, from the first stroke of the pencil—was lost. Organizational and disciplinary barriers worked against its rediscovery. Absorber development was a small and arcane branch of elec-

Construction of the Horten HoXVIII long-range bomber actually started in April 1945. The six-jet bomber, carrying half its weight in fuel, was designed to have a range of no less than 7,400 miles with an 8,000 pound bombload. H. Weishaupt Verlag

trical engineering, carried out in small laboratories. Electrical and aeronautical engineers spoke different languages; absorber people would talk enthusiastically of "imaginary parts to the dielectric constant" and the aircraft designers' eyes would glaze over.

Spying

The first move to break the jam came from a user group; not from the fighter or bomber pilots, but the strategic reconnaissance community. It was the British military intelligence organization, in the years before the 1939-45 war, which set the risky precedent of sponsoring illegal and covert reconnaissance flights over a potential adversary's territory in peacetime. After the outbreak of war, the operation became an official and immensely valuable RAF unit, operating in parallel with USAAF reconnaissance squadrons. After 1945, with barely a decent interval, RAF and USAAF aircraft began to probe the military secrets of their former ally, the Soviet Union. Converted bombers were used at first, but these were too vulnerable for operations over the central Soviet Union, where most of the important military developments and much production took place.

Late in 1952, USAF Major John Seaberg, a professional aeronautical engineer, started work on a design concept for an aircraft intended to plug the reconnaissance gap. It would combine a new-generation turbojet with a low-airspeed, high-altitude airframe, and would be capable of cruising at 70,000 feet. This was some miles higher than the world's absolute altitude record, set by a fighter in an all-out climb which

ended when the aircraft ran out of airspeed. In March 1953, a specification was drafted for such an aircraft, including the requirement that "consideration will be given . . . to minimize the detectability by enemy radar."

This requirement was logical. The spyplane would operate alone at high altitude, and at that time no aircraft smaller than a bomber could carry its own active jamming equipment.

There was another good reason for requiring reduced detectability. Intelligence is most valuable when the subject is unaware that it has been obtained. It is the work of minutes to push a secret prototype airplane back into its hangar, and the work of seconds to shut down a sensitive transmission, so the quality of

Clarence L. "Kelly" Johnson's renowned Skunk Works rose to fame by developing radical, high-performance aircraft, such as the F-104 Starfighter, in complete secrecy.

One of the first "black" airplane programs in peacetime produced the Lockheed U-2, designed for covert (and illegal) flights over the Soviet Union. Lockheed

intelligence gathered by any system depends to some extent on its detectability.

U-2

The process that started with Seaberg's requirement resulted in the development of the first aircraft designed expressly for illegal reconnaissance activities. The Lockheed U-2 was the brainchild of Lockheed's legendary chief engineer, Clarence L. "Kelly" Johnson. His belief, backed up by results on the P-80 and F-104 fighters, was that advanced aircraft should be designed and built by small teams of hand-picked people, working to meet a mission statement, rather than a specification. An organization known as Advanced Development Projects (ADP) was set up along these lines at Burbank.

The small size of the ADP operation made it possible to achieve a very high degree of secrecy, which also isolated the team from outside interference. Those without the need and clearance to know were barred from the ADP office and prototype shop, with ruthless impartiality. Lockheed people began to call it the Skunk Works, after the moonshine factory in the *L'il Abner* comic strip, and the name stuck despite high-level disapproval.

The U-2 made its first flight in August 1955 and sustained one of the most successful intelligence programs in history. A testimony to its design is that, although the Air Force wanted an ultra-light, short-life aircraft, one of the first U-2s was still gathering earth-resources data for NASA in early 1988.

As it turned out, the design of the U-2 was little influenced by the call for low RCS, which had become one of those "nice-to-have" design features which must sometimes be sacrificed to meet basic mission requirements. But the design process had introduced the reconnaissance community to the idea of reduced detectability, and the Skunk Works to the reconnaissance community. And this proved, in the long run, to be very important.

From the start of the U-2 program, it was accepted that the U-2 would not be able to penetrate Soviet airspace indefinitely. The first effort to produce a replacement involved a massive hydrogen-fueled aircraft, the Lockheed L-400. It was abandoned for many sound reasons, but one look at its design confirms that it would have been a huge radar target compared to the U-2. After this false start, a completely fresh approach was made.

This time, reduced detectabiliy was a much higher priority than it had been in the design of the U-2, because the new spyplane was to be very fast and, inevitably, much bigger than the U-2. Unless the detectability was kept under control, the benefits of higher performance would be diluted, because hostile radars could detect and track the new aircraft at longer range.

A-12 Oxcart

In August 1959, Lockheed was selected to develop the new aircraft, after a design competition with General Dynamics. Code-named Oxcart, Lockheed's design was a conventional delta-winged aircraft about the size of a B-58, with two turbo-ramjet engines (powerplants based on conventional turbojets, but integrated with complex inlet, bypass and nozzle systems so that they took on the characteristics of a ramjet at high speeds).

Flown in April 1962, the Lockheed A-12 was the first aircraft in which the basic design was affected by the needs of low observables.

The "chines" on the forebody, nacelle-to-wing blending and inward-canted fins were all intended to reduce reflectivity. Lockheed

The performance goals for the new aircraft were as far ahead of most previous work as those of the U-2 had been: low detectability was vital, but it had to be achieved without reducing performance. The Skunk Works team recognized—perhaps for the first time since the HoIX—that the only way to do this was to address the issue from the start

The A-12, developed for the CIA, evolved into the heavier, two-seater SR-71. Originally developed as a reconnaissance-strike aircraft for SAC, to be armed with SRAMs or MK43 bombs, the SR-71 was never tested with weapons and the fuselage bays were used for reconnaissance equipment. Lockheed

of design work, through the basic configuration. The result was that the Oxcart design—designated A-12 by Lockheed and the CIA, and later developed into the YF-12A experimental interceptor and the SR-71 Blackbird reconnaissance/strike aircraft—looked startlingly different from any other aircraft of the time. Although the YF-12A was unveiled in March 1964 (about two years after the A-12's maiden flight) it was almost two decades before many of its RCS-related subtleties could be appreciated outside a small and tight-lipped circle.

While most military aircraft in the sixties were slab-sided and jagged in shape, the A-12 was made up of a few long, straight lines and a great many curves. Kelly Johnson has compared the front view of the airplane to "a snake swallowing three mice." The thin delta wing is smoothly blended into the slender oval-section fuselage and the two big engine nacelles. From directly above or below, the airplane seems much larger than it does from the side, because the fuselage is flared out into broad, shallow "chines" which run all the way to the nose. The two vertical fins, leaning inward, seem small, particularly when one looks at the two vast engines set far out on the wings. If one engine fails, the other creates a powerful turning moment.

It all seemed needlessly complex to most experts of the day. "The basic layout with engines mid-mounted on a slender delta will stick in the throats of some fighter manufacturers," British aviation magazine *Flying Review* commented, [and] "it goes against the grain to waste wetted area and bend the spars around the powerplant." The anonymous author further described the wing-mounted engines as "an aerodynamically retrograde step." The magazine also wondered aloud why the aircraft was painted black.

In fact, reduced RCS was the hidden driver behind many of the design features. Moving the engines into separate mid-wing pods meant that the aircraft would be as small as possible from the side and the front, the angles from which it was most likely to be observed. The complex blending eliminated verti-

cal plane surfaces from the shape, so that incoming radar waves would strike the airplane at an oblique angle. The canting of the vertical fins served the same purpose. There was a price for many of these features. Without large vertical fins or auxiliary belly fins, the A-12 was unstable at high speed, and a complex, double-redundant automatic pilot had to be developed to make it flyable and safe. The structure was complex, as the British writer had noted, and special fabrication techniques had to be developed in many instances.

The edges of the SR-71's wings are notched to accept wedges of radar-absorbent material, a plastic honeycomb developed by Lockheed.

The notches provide a good geometry for absorption, combined with structural strength.

The A-12 was black because it was covered with a paint-type RAM incorporating ferrite particles in an epoxy base. It provided useful absorption for a negligible increase in weight and drag. Under the A-12's skin, radar-absorbent plastic material was used on the wing leading edges and control surfaces. At least one A-12 had plastic-skinned chines, and all-plastic vertical fins were also tested. The plastic fins were not standardized, because they did not make much difference to the RCS.

The value of the RCS-reduction measures applied to the A-12 has been debatable, mainly because the type's performance in other respects was so high. The A-12 and SR-71 have a sustained cruising speed of Mach 3.5 (2,300 mph) and can maintain a height of 95,000 feet. Because they are designed

Like the SR-71, this U-2R is painted with a polymer-based material containing tiny ferrite particles which absorb radar energy and give it the name "iron ball." Lockheed

to refuel in flight several times during a sortie, they possess virtually global range. They were frequently detected and attacked in operations over North Vietnam and China between 1967 and 1972, but the available missiles were simply too slow and cumbersome to arrive within lethal distance. Even in the early 1980s, it was felt that the only system that could touch the SR-71 was the massive SA-5 *Griffon* missile, and that even then the weapon's accuracy would be so poor that only a thermonuclear warhead would kill the target.

Drones

It was no fault of Lockheed that the A-12 came too late to continue the immensely valuable Soviet overflight reconnaissance operation, which ended when Francis Gary Powers' U-2 was shot down over Sverdlovsk on May 1, 1960. Politics and diplomacy dictated the abandonment of manned overflights, but the decision was made easier by the fact that reconnaissance satellites, safe from interference in the no-man's-land of space, could provide some intelligence data. At least the planners would no longer have to work in an absolute vacuum, as they had before 1955.

Nobody, however, could believe that reconnaissance satellites would fill every need. Satellites were expensive and slow to launch, so that they could not respond quickly to national needs. Their sensors were further from their objectives and some forms of data collection (radar and infrared, for example) were not practical. The satellite had a limited life, and its sensors were lost with it when it re-entered the atmosphere and burnt up. Finally, getting large quantities of data (such as high-resolution imagery) out of a satellite was difficult in the early sixties; the only way to do it was to jettison a recoverable film capsule. The need for airborne reconnaissance systems was still there; but the risk to the pilot, in the era of SAMs, could not be ignored. Unlike the bomber, a strategic reconnaissance aircraft could not accomplish its mission at 200 feet.

Q-2 Firebee and Hound Dog

But there was one way to eliminate the risk to the reconnaissance pilot: leave him behind. Before Gary Powers' ill-fated Sverdlovsk mission, the Ryan Aeronautical company had briefed the USAF on the reconnaissance potential of the Q-2 Firebee target drone, and had offered a version which would be "virtually undetectable" by radar. The program gained a surge of speed after May 1, and a research contract was issued in July—one week after another US reconnaissance aircraft had been shot down over the Barents Sea.

Part of the program included ground tests of model Q-2s with paint-type RAM on the nose, a form of flexible RAM bonded to the fuselage sides and a wire-mesh screen over the undernose air intake. In September 1960, flight tests of a similarly modified Q-2 showed a useful decrease in RCS.

This was not the only such program under way. In 1960, for example, the USAF issued a contract to North American to reduce the RCS of the AGM-28B Hound Dog air-to-surface missile. While these efforts might suggest that RAM alone could reduce the radar reflectivity of an aircraft, it should be remembered that the Q-2 and AGM-28B were much

smaller than any manned combat aircraft.

Model 136

Meanwhile, Ryan pushed ahead with the design of the Model 136, a true covert, high-altitude reconnaissance drone. The underside of the aircraft (which was all that a surveillance radar would see) was almost perfectly flat. The engine inlet and exhaust were on top of the fuselage, shielded from radar and infrared detectors, and the fins were canted inward like those of the A-12.

The program was on the point of going ahead, under the code name Red Wagon, at the time of the November

This Ryan Q-2C drone was equipped with RAM blankets (the dark areas on the fuselage) and a wire-mesh fairing over the nose inlet. The fine mesh blocked radar waves out of the inlet duct. These modified drones proved almost impossible to track using contemporary fighter radars. Teledyne Ryan Aeronautical

By 1967, the modified Q-2 had become the Model 147T, making extensive use of built-in RAM, rather than heavy blankets, to defeat radar. Evidence of the use of RAM and surface treatments is seen in the dark areas of the wing, nose and tail, and in the large wing fillets which give some of the advantages of wing-body blending. Thirty-three surviving Model 147Ts. stored in the mid-seventies, were sold to Israel in 1984. Teledyne Ryan Aeronautical

1960 presidential election. Opponents of the system, including some USAF people who saw it as a threat to the manned Oxcart, took advantage of the period between the Republicans' loss of the election and President John F. Kennedy's inauguration to kill the project.

Lucy Lee

Ryan tried again in 1961 with the Lucy Lee, a larger drone for "peripheral" signals intelligence missions, but was turned down in early 1962. However, drone supporters in the USAF managed to secure funding for a continued research program using modified Q-2s with cameras, built-in navigation systems and RAM. In March 1962, one of

the "treated" Q-2s was launched from a C-130 over Tyndall AFB, Florida, and five of the Air Defense Command's then-new F-106 interceptors, carrying live AIM-4 Falcon missiles, were sent out to destroy it. Ground radar picked up the target, and the pilots saw its contrail, but the fighter radars could not lock on to it and the Falcon missiles would not guide.

Model 147

Together with good reconnaissance results (accurate, high-resolution imagery) the low vulnerability demonstrated by the Model 147 drones persuaded the USAF to continue the program. In 1964, the drones were tested operationally over mainland China. Eventually, a bewildering series of Model 147 subtypes was built and operated, and the Lightning Bugs, as they were called, were a major asset to photographic and electronic reconnaissance operations over Vietnam.

Early operational versions were not usually "treated" and many were shot down by SAMs, including four by Chinese SA-2s. Even so, they proved difficult targets for fighters, and brought back a great deal of intelligence. Later versions of the series, such as the re-engined, long-span Model 147T, were equipped with an array of radar-absorbent components known as HIDE (high-absorbency integrated defense), to reduce radar reflection from the engine and airframe.

D-21 and Compass Arrow

Despite the failure of the Red Wagon program to gain approval in 1960, the idea of a low-observables unmanned strategic reconnaissance system remained alive. By September 1961, seven major manufacturers had proposed such systems, two were developed and tested and, ultimately, one was placed in service. More than fifteen years after the programs ended, details of both are still largely classified.

One of these was a very high speed, expendable drone. Designated D-21, it was developed by the Lockheed Missiles & Space Company in collaboration with the Skunk Works, and is believed to have started flight tests in 1966. It was powered by a Marquardt RJ43 ramjet engine (these were obtained from USAF/Boeing Bomarc missiles, which had been taken out of service) and was designed to be launched at almost Mach 3 from a piggy-back pylon on an A-12. The drone itself could cruise at Mach 3.8, well above 100,000 feet. Its range is classified but was well over 2,000 miles.

In its planform and profile, the D-21 resembled an A-12 nacelle and two A-12 outer wings. It was highly blended, with room for reconnaissance sensor bays on either side of the ramjet duct. Data was

Teledyne Ryan's AQM-91A Compass Arrow was the first large aircraft specifically designed to survive by Stealth. Two AQM-91s are seen here beneath a DC-130E, showing *their size, their flat underside and their small, inward-canted fins.* Teledyne Ryan Aeronautical

stored in an ejectable capsule, to be recovered by a midair snatch operation at the end of the reconnaissance run. (This operation proved more difficult than in the case of the more predictable satellite, and was never very reliable.) It is believed that the airframe used considerable amounts of RAM, and the ramjet tailpipe was extended to mask the infrared signature from the engine.

The other low-observable drone of this era was developed by Ryan under the Compass Arrow program, and bore a strong resemblance to the canceled Model 136 proposal. Designated Model 154 by the company and AQM-91A by the USAF, it was ordered in 1966 and

flew in 1969. Like the Model 136, it had a flat underside, a dorsal engine shielded by the fuselage and twin inward-canted fins. It was a large aircraft, powered by an 8,000 pound thrust General Electric J97 engine with a specially developed mixer nozzle. This drone's intended mission was never discussed, but it was probably designed to take over from the extensively modified high-altitude Firebee drones, which were at greater risk from SAMs than the low-level versions.

Both Compass Arrow and the D-21 were still under development in 1972, when President Richard Nixon visited Beijing and agreed to halt overflights to mainland China. Both the D-21 and the

The AQM-91A was powered by a General Electric J97 with a dorsal inlet and exhaust, fitted with a special mixer nozzle and shielded by the fuselage and the horizontal and vertical tail surfaces. Like other reconnaissance drones, the AQM-91A was recovered by parachute and "snatched" in midair by a helicopter. Teledyne Ryan Aeronautical

AQM-91A were thereby robbed of their primary missions, and both programs were terminated in the period 1972-73.

Lockheed YO-3A

One other low-observables aircraft had been developed for the Vietnam war. One of the main problems in that conflict was tracking an enemy who could move large forces and substantial amounts of equipment at night, through dense jungle trails, mainly on foot and by bicycle. Normal methods of air observation were impossible because there was little, if any, engine sound on the ground to mask the sound of a reconnaissance aircraft overhead. In 1966, the Defense Advanced Research Projects Agency (DARPA), a Pentagon organization charged with pursuing advanced projects which lay outside service experience, picked up the requirement and, in 1966, funded a Lockheed program to develop such an aircraft.

After a number of experiments, Lockheed eventually produced fourteen YO-3A reconnaissance aircraft. The YO-3A was based on a Schweizer sailplane, although little more than the wing and tail remained. It was powered by a modified lightplane engine, with a long exhaust pipe which ended in a long muffler mounted on the fuselage side, and had a large, slow-turning, six-blade wooden propeller driven by rubber belts. While the end of the Vietnam war meant the end of the YO-3A's mission, it has the distinction of being the first manned combat aircraft designed to survive a hostile environment by no other means than reduced observability.

By 1972, a great deal had been accomplished in the world of reduced observables. Flyable low-RCS configurations had been developed and used as the basis for practical reconnaissance systems. Progress had been demonstrated in the difficult area of manufacturing efficient radar-absorbent structures. Particularly important were the successful tests of the Lockheed D-21 and the Teledyne Ryan AQM-91A, be-

Another aircraft designed to complete its mission undetected—and, like the D-21, developed by Lockheed—was the YO-3A quiet reconnaissance aircraft used by the US Army in Vietnam. Note the broad-chord three-blade propeller and prominent mufflers. A similar vehicle was produced in 1986 by Schweizer Aircraft. Lockheed

Even less obtrusive than the YO-3 was the experimental Q-Star, with a liquid-cooled engine buried in the rear fuselage for more effective silencing. Lockheed

This very normal looking little aircraft, the Windecker YE-5A, was used by the USAF and Lockheed for a series of classified tests in the early days of the Stealth program. Because of its all-fiberglass airframe, it could be treated with internal RAM and brought down to a very low RCS. Dr. Leo Windecker

cause these vehicles, nearly as large as a small fighter such as the Northrop F-5, had demonstrated reduced observability at full scale. Finally, a manned combat aircraft successfully used reduced observables to meet an otherwise difficult requirement.

It would have been surprising if nobody had thought of applying such techniques to a more potent warplane. In early 1988, Northrop stated that its work on low observables had started as far back as the mid-sixties. The same could probably be said for Lockheed's Skunk Works. Nevertheless, the number of people aware of the potential of low observables was small. They also believed that the concept was so important that its details should be kept from any adversary. As a result, the security curtain which the reconnaissance community and the Skunk Works had imposed on low-observables work was never lifted.

Linebacker

The end of extensive air operations in the Vietnam war sent shock waves through the aerospace industry, as production contracts were cut back. Some companies, such as Rockwell and McDonnell Douglas, had secured big development contracts for new warplanes; others, including Lockheed, were in much more delicate shape. The Burbank company was afflicted with prob-

Another advanced reconnaissance system was the D-21 drone. Sharing many features with the SR-71, the D-21 is thought to have made even more extensive use of radar-absorbent materials and other Stealth features. Jay Miller/Aerofax

Side view of a D-21 shows its slender profile, blending between the vertical fin and the body, and what appears to be a radar-absorbent blanket on its upper surface. The

long tailpipe may have been designed to suppress the IR signature from the Marquardt RJ43 ramjet engine. Jay Miller/ Aerofax

lems on all fronts. The TriStar airliner, into which the company had plowed its Vietnam-era earnings, was behind schedule and over cost, because Rolls-Royce, the builder of its engines, had gone bankrupt. Lockheed had agreed to build the C-5 freighter at a fixed price, had experienced cost overruns and was trying to renegotiate the contract at a reduced but still staggering loss. The AH-56 strike helicopter was at the point of being canceled, partly because of technical problems but mainly because the Army had changed its mind about what sort of helicopter it wanted. The Skunk Works had problems as well; SR-

71 production had ended and ADP had nothing to follow it.

As the saying goes, necessity is the mother of invention: it was around this difficult time, in 1972 or 1973, that the Skunk Works proposed that the new technology of low observables should be applied to the problems of conventional air warfare rather than reconnaissance.

When the USAF started to bomb North Vietnam, it had gone after small targets such as bridges and power plants as it had been training to do for years, with fighter aircraft laden with bombs, flying low at maximum speed. It soon became clear that small targets could

Originally designed for launch from an A-12 or SR-71, the D-21 was modified for launch from the B-52H after the Mach 3 launch was found to be too dangerous. A fuel tank and rocket booster were added beneath the fuselage. Lockheed

not be hit with bombs from such altitudes, and that more accurate dive attacks were suicidal in the face of radar-directed anti-aircraft artillery (AAA), let alone the SA-2 missiles which were introduced in July 1965.

The USAF's response was to surround its tactical bombers with an ever-expanding phalanx of specially equipped aircraft, dedicated to destroying, distracting or degrading the defensive weapons in the bombers' path. The final raids over North Vietnam were the two Linebacker operations of 1972, aimed at Hanoi and Haiphong. A Linebacker strike could include seventy aircraft, of which only a minority carried bombs. The balance of the force included fighter escorts and aircraft dedicated to electronic warfare. These included bombers carrying nothing but chaff (strands of metalized fiberglass, resembling a poor-quality blond wig), which created false echoes on the defensive radar screens. The chaff escorts had a dangerous job, because they naturally flew in front of this electronic smokescreen. Other support aircraft included B-66 bombers, laden with high-powered jamming equipment, and Wild Weasel aircraft, fitted with specially developed electronic systems and loaded with missiles which homed on to hostile radars. Every aircraft which could do so carried its own jamming pod.

The Linebacker missions were successful, in terms of both results and loss rates. The immense resources devoted to EW, however, could hardly pass unnoticed, and neither could the magnitude of the risks involved in such tasks as electronic intelligence (mapping the defenses before a strike) and chaff bombing. It was recognized, too, that the electronic battle had been close-run, and that the most modern Soviet missiles had not been deployed. It would not have taken a quantum leap in technology to shift the battle decisively against the attacker, and the USAF knew it.

SAM developments

It was also known that the Soviet Union was placing a great deal of emphasis on the SAM, developing more new systems than the US and deploying them in larger numbers. Most of the new weapons were mounted on tracked vehicles, so the SAM belts would be harder to map than they had been in Vietnam. A good example of this trend was the SA-6 *Gainful* missile, which was first seen in a Red Square parade in 1967. A tracked amphibious vehicle carried three missiles ready to fire; the weapon itself had a rocket/ramjet engine, so that it would be powered and maneuverable even at the end of its flight. It was known to be teamed with a mobile radar system, but that was not on display in Moscow; indeed, its characteristics were a closely guarded secret.

In October 1973, war broke out in the Middle East. Those who expected a rerun of June 1967, when the Israeli air force swarmed over its adversaries and decided the war in minutes, were in for a shock. The Egyptian armed forces had been equipped with the new SA-6, and rapidly deployed the missiles forward to cover their advancing troops and supply lines. Better jammers were rushed to the scene by the United States and, together with improved tactics, these turned the tide against the SA-6. But the losses suf-

The combat debut of the SA-6 missile system, in the October 1973 Arab-Israeli war, was a major shock for the West, and spurred the development of aircraft which could survive against any radar-guided SAM systems. US Department of Defense

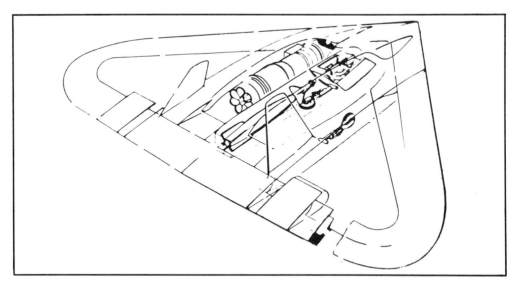

This study for a Tactical High-Altitude Penetrator (THAP) aircraft was prepared by a bunch of the USAF's Aeronautical Systems Division, and was released in 1980. It is a flying wing with two buried turbofan engines and a deep layer of RAM—comprising nonconducting skins and foam cores—extending around its entire perimeter. The canted vertical fins, called rudderatorons, provide pitch, roll and yaw control in cruising flight. USAF via Interavia

fered in the first few hours of combat by one of the world's best trained and best equipped air forces were sobering.

In the following year, the Skunk Works was funded to start work on a prototype of its proposed low-observables strike aircraft. A brief report, not attributed to any source, appeared in *Aviation Week*. For most people in the · aerospace business and for everybody outside it, it was the first time they had heard of a new technology called "Stealth."

Lockheed's Stealth demonstration program is believed to have been funded by DARPA, under the codename Have Blue. The aircraft was also known as the XST (experimental, Stealth, tactical). Several prototypes were built at Burbank between 1975 and 1977, and were then ferried by truck or C-5 freighter into Nevada.

Their destination was Groom Lake, a flight-test and final assembly facility which had been established in 1955 to test the U-2. The dry Groom Lake lies within the vast Air Force weapons and practice range, covering an area the size of Switzerland, which extends in the shape of an inverted triangle to the north of Nellis AFB, which itself is outside Las Vegas. Surrounded by mountains, Groom Lake was chosen because it is invisible to any ground-level observer outside the Nellis range, and because the dry lake provided a ready foundation for concrete runways and, as at Edwards AFB, a long strip for emergency landings.

Starting out as a collection of temporary huts in the fifties, Groom expanded with the programs which were located there. The A-12 was tested from Groom; far more complex than the U-2, and ranging farther afield on its test flights, the Blackbird required much more extensive maintenance, checkout and data-processing facilities. By the early seventies, Groom had become a second Edwards AFB, and one of the most secret and best protected sites in any democratic nation.

The entire Nellis range is ringed with electronic detectors; security teams in helicopters respond rapidly to any intrusion. Groom Lake itself is a citadel within a fortress. Pilots practicing on the range are forbidden to overfly Groom Lake or to pay too much attention to any unidentifiable aircraft they may see in flight. Nellis is also an intensive airborne training area, under constant radar surveillance down to ground level, so the ban on civilian air traffic can be rigorously enforced.

F-117A

Designed and developed under the leadership of Ben Rich, the first XST flew in 1977, followed by a number of others. The primary mission of these aircraft was to verify the low-observable qualities of the design, in flight and at full scale; performance, handling and compliance with standard military specifications were of secondary importance.

Validating RCS to the minute degree of accuracy required by Stealth is something which cannot be done on small-scale models. And large-scale outdoor RCS measuring ranges are compromises at best, and even then cannot simulate dynamic RCS phenomena such as those caused by flexing of the aircraft structure in flight. Approaches to reducing detectability in the visual, acoustic and

Lockheed's F-117A was revealed by the USAF in November 1988. Its external surface is "faceted," consisting of many flat surfaces. It is said to "fly better than it looks" which is not saying a great deal. USAF

thermal spectra were also demonstrated. The test program was generally successful despite the loss of one aircraft in 1977; veteran Lockheed pilot Bill Parks was injured when his seat failed to separate after ejection.

In 1978, the Carter administration authorized the development by Lockheed of an operational Stealth fighter. It was to be designed for precise, covert attacks, with minimal collateral damage, on high-value targets in any theater. The program was code-named Senior Trend, following a pattern set by earlier ADP programs such as Senior Crown (SR-71) and Senior Bowl (D-21). Later, it was given the designation F-117A, continuing a sequence of designations which had been used to cover the captured Soviet MiG fighters flown by the USAF's secret "Red Hat" squadron.

The first F-117A flew in June 1981, and the type became operational in October 1983, at a brand-new air base on the site of an airstrip on the Tonopah Test Range, a weapons range that abuts

the northwestern corner of the Nellis complex. A new unit, the 4450th Tactical Group, was formed to operate the aircraft, manned by highly experienced strike pilots with F-111 or Wild Weasel experience.

However, the Pentagon refused to acknowledge the fighter's existence until November 1988. Basic and quite consistent descriptions of the XST and F-117A circulated throughout the early years of the program. All of them were inaccurate. The problem is the same one which faced the medieval artist in his attempts to depict a rhinoceros, on the basis of a second-hand verbal description. In such circumstances, the mind's eye is drawn toward the familiar, and the artist ends up drawing a unicorn.

In fact, the F-117A is about the size of an F-4 or F-18, but has a very different shape. The planform is an arrowhead, the leading edges being straight from the wingtips to the nose (in this respect, the F-117A resembles the B-2), and the center-section being extended rearward. There is a distinct division in front view between the short body and the swept outer wings, which are removable to permit the aircraft to be transported in a C-5A. The pointed tail of the body section supports a small V-tail.

The body is squat and almost pyramidical. Its surface comprises many small, perfectly flat facets, which may take the form of RAM bonded to the substructure. A canopy composed of flat panes and thick frames forms the apex of the pyramid. The body accommodates the single pilot, two engines (generally believed to be GE F404s, without afterburner), weapons, landing gear and much of the fuel.

The wingspan appears to be around forty-five feet, and overall length is under thirty feet. This, and the amount of power available, suggest a gross weight in the vicinity of 45,000 pounds. The weapon load may be around 4,000 pounds, and is reported to be carried in two bays, which is not surprising, because the length of a centerline bay would be restricted by the cockpit.

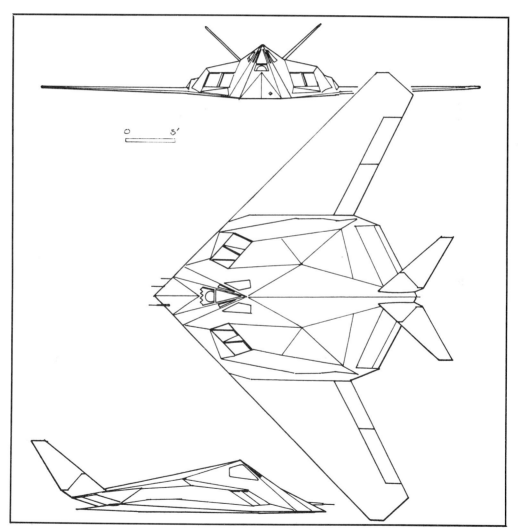

The F-117A is not a true flying wing, but has a short, broad body terminating in a V-tail. It has a wingspan of around 45 feet, and is about the same size as an A-7. There are two weapon bays, one on either side of the cockpit. A sensor of some kind appears to be mounted ahead of the windshield.

Blending and faceting give the F-117A a hump-backed, reptilian appearance. It has been said that the Boeing XB-47 was "a sacred airplane" because the usual comment of a visitor seeing the then-secret mock-up for the first time was "Holy Christ!" Eyewitness descriptions of first encounters with the F-117A sound much the same. According to a report in *Time* magazine, the F-117A is nicknamed the Wobbly Goblin by its pilots.

Performance numbers must be rule-of-thumb estimates at best, but it can be confidently stated that the F-117A is subsonic. Neither its wing loading, configuration nor thrust/weight ratio suggests a high degree of agility.

The aircraft has been described as "flying better than it looks," but this could be a case of damning with faint praise. Its acceleration is not sparkling, and because of its wing loading and configuration it becomes stable (and relatively slow in maneuver) at high speed and low level.

In terms of range, however, the F-117A may yield to few aircraft of its size. In 1987, *The New York Times* reported that USMC Lieutenant Colonel Oliver North prepared a plan to use the F-117A in a strike against Libya's Colonel Khaddafi. (It was vetoed by the Joint Chiefs of Staff on the grounds that the F-117A should not be risked on such a mission.) North apparently proposed that the F-

This base of Tonopah, Nevada, was built specifically to accommodate the F-117A squadron. Las Vegas Review-Journal

117A be ferried to Rota, near Cadiz, for the attack. It is approximately 1,200 nautical miles over water from Rota to Tripoli, equivalent to the distance from RAF Kinloss to Leningrad or Murmansk, from Eastern England to Kiev, from Kadena AB (Okinawa) to Vladivostok, or almost anywhere in the Middle East from Pakistan or Turkey.

This impressive range is made credible by the F-117A's large internal fuel capacity, the absence of external stores and its relatively small, non-afterburning efficient engines. Another important factor is that the aircraft can cruise at any altitude without increasing the range at which a defensive system will detect it.

A total of fifty-nine F-117s have been ordered, of which seven remained to be delivered in November 1988. The last aircraft will be delivered in fiscal year 1990, so the rate presumably peaked at ten aircraft per year. The total produced may be less than the original plan, for a number of reasons. The aircraft is believed to be expensive, largely because of the extremely high precision in manufacture which LO aircraft demand. (The entire program is said to have cost $7 billion, including research and development.) It is also highly specialized, with a small weapons load, and is optimized to attack a small set of specific, high-value targets such as command and control centers, strategic bridges, weapons dumps, large missile sites and so on. By the nineties, some of its missions could be undertaken by the B-2 or the US Navy's A-12, which represent a newer generation of LO technology.

Three of the aircraft have been lost in accidents, one of which occurred near Bakersfield, California, on July 11, 1986. Another fatal F-117A accident occurred on the Nellis range in October 1987.

According to *The New York Times*, the F-117A has been deployed to Britain on a number of occasions. Presumably as part of the same agreement, at least one RAF pilot has been attached to the 4450th TG. However, the unit also uses eighteen LTV A-7D Corsairs as "surrogate trainers" in order to train outside Nellis during daylight hours, and to make deployments to other USAF bases and to foreign bases without costly security measures. The aircraft are modified with some components of the F-117A navigation attack system, including a sensor pod. The subsonic, non-afterburning A-7D, with its moderate wing loading and low thrust/weight ratio, also resembles the F-117A in its acceleration, speed and maneuvering envelope.

Forthcoming tactical Stealth aircraft such as the Advanced Tactical Fighter and the A-12 will offer similar low-observable characteristics to those of the F-117A, at a much lower cost in dollars and performance. When the full story of the F-117A and Senior Trend is written, many years hence, it will be seen as a landmark like the first jet fighters or the first supersonic fighters; not perfect, but first. The XST program, in particular, was a powerful influence on planning from the start of its flight tests. As it turned out, the first XST took to the air at a time when Strategic Air Command's bomber plans were, once again, in a state of flux.

Chapter 3

The Gigabuck Zone

A billion here, a billion there, and pretty soon you're talking real money.

Senator Everett M. Dirksen

Dogged by budget cuts and threatened by high-level debate over the rationale for the manned bomber, the B-1 battled its way toward its objectives in the early seventies. The Palmdale factory where Rockwell was to have built the B-70 was refurbished to assemble the aircraft. The program already meant thousands of jobs to Californians, but no one company could build the whole system. As the design took shape, major sub-contracts were placed with Boeing, in Seattle; with Vought in Texas; with AIL/Cutler-Hammer in Long Island, and hundreds of others.

Funding dilemma

The first B-1 was rolled out at Palmdale in October 1974, and made its first flight on December 23. Gleaming white with a natty black radome, it was a devilishly elegant aircraft. However, the program was already in trouble on two counts: underestimation of costs and budget cuts.

A problem which seems common to all new weapons is higher-than-estimated cost. Actually, it is a problem common to virtually all projects that involve unknowns, from remodeling a kitchen in an old house to building a large bridge or developing a new computer. The difference between weapon system overruns and similar occurrences in the private sector is that the amounts involved are larger, and a matter of public record.

To underestimate is human when the chances of getting a project approved vary inversely with the predicted cost, which they usually do. It is also as impractical to take the "worst case" scenario as the basis for a program as it is to assume that nothing will go wrong at all. Planning for the worst case simply guarantees that the project will take longer and cost more to carry out than if a "middle case" had been projected and achieved.

Another way to reduce risk is to complete the development stage before

64

spending any money on production. Again, this guarantees that the project will take longer and cost more (the two go hand in hand) than it would have if some degree of "concurrency" between development and production had been accepted. Neither does it eliminate the risk of overruns in development.

In the case of the B-1, the cost increases in the early stages of development—or, more to the point, the underestimation of costs before development started—stemmed from the fact that the aircraft was neither the biggest in the world, nor the fastest. It was about the size of a 707 jetliner, and its flight performance was similar to that of the F-111. Many of its features, such as the terrain-following radar and escape capsule for the crew, were similar to those of the F-111. It was therefore not regarded as a high-risk design, or particularly difficult to design and build. However, its combination of size and high performance was unique. Among other things, this very large aircraft would be as densely packed as a small fighter—with electronic equipment, wiring, hydraulic lines and structural members.

In an earlier era, Rockwell and the USAF would have damned the torpedoes and maintained the original targets. However, budget restrictions were a reality in the seventies, and the risk was that the B-1 would monopolize production funding and leave too little money for important aircraft such as the F-15 fighter. Under pressure, the

Rockwell's B-1 was designed to combine low-level, high-subsonic penetration with Mach 2 speed at high altitude. The white markings on the nose of this aircraft were added because the B-1's smooth shape gave no visual cues to refueling boom operators; at normal air-combat ranges, they are not visible.
Rockwell

USAF was forced to eliminate some features from the aircraft to make it less costly to build. The variable-geometry engine inlets were replaced by fixed inlets. This was a particularly serious change, because it meant that the bomber would never attain anything like the Mach 2.2 maximum speed in the original specification. (Critics had argued that supersonic dash would use so much fuel

USAF plans for a new bomber were given a valuable boost, late in 1969, by the revelation that the Soviet Union was developing a new long-range combat aircraft. This eventually entered service as the Tupolev Tu-22M Backfire. US Department of Defense

A major reason for the cancellation of the B-1A production program was the promise of this weapon, the USAF/Boeing AGM-86B Air-Launched Cruise Missile (ALCM). Most of the body is a fuel tank, the guidance system and warhead occupying the nose section. US Department of Defense

that the B-1 would hardly ever use that corner of the flight envelope.) Also eliminated was the crew escape capsule, in favor of conventional ejection seats. The problem with downgrading requirements, however, was that it resurrected the question of why the B-52 had to be replaced at all.

Budget cuts

The second big problem for the B-1 resulted indirectly from the budget cuts. Early in the program, the USAF had proposed to equip the B-1 with a decoy like the B-52's Quail, but which would carry a small nuclear warhead so that it could not be ignored even if it were identified. Boeing was given a contract to develop this device, which was designated the ADM-86 SCAD (subsonic cruise armed decoy). In 1973 the USAF canceled SCAD as such, but funded continued studies of the system as a potential weapon for the B-52. That decision was to haunt the B-1.

Rather than being a smaller "Mk2" Quail, the AGM-86 (as it was now designated) began to emerge as a new strategic weapon, a cruise missile, incorporating a blend of new features that had not been foreseen when the B-1 was launched. There were two critical technologies involved: guidance and propulsion. The missile was guided by an inertial navigation system, coupled to a radar altimeter which would measure the ground profile below the missile at a pre-set point and compare it with a pre-programmed matrix of ground heights in the same area. It could therefore determine its position within that area and correct the inertial platform. The weapon would be much more accurate than any previous cruise missile. Because it was accurate, the new cruise missile would not need the heavy megaton-range warheads required by older cruise missiles such as the Hound Dog.

Propulsion was the other key technology. It had been axiomatic that small jet engines were less efficient than big ones. One man who did not believe this

Unlike a man-carrying bomber, the ALCM was designed for a flying life measured in hours and could be built rapidly and cheaply, using many castings in place of expensive machined components. At the program's peak, Boeing produced 40 missiles per month. Boeing

was Dr. Sam Williams, founder of Williams Research (later Williams International). By the late sixties, Williams Research was testing its WR19, a turbofan with a potential 600 pound thrust rating which consumed only 0.7 pounds of fuel per pound of thrust per hour.

The original Boeing AGM-86 emerged as an accurate missile with a range of 750 miles, but no bigger than SRAM. However, this was only part of the story. By stretching the body and uprating the engine, the weapon's range could be increased to 1,500 miles. A B-52 could carry twenty such weapons and launch them from outside the Soviet landmass. The first cruise missile prototypes were launched in March 1976 as the presidential election was heating up.

The ax falls . . .

The B-1 continued to survive votes in Congress, by a narrow margin, and in December 1976 the Department of Defense approved production of 240 B-1s. The first of these would be delivered in 1979 and become operational in mid-1982. But the timing made it clear that this was merely a gesture by the lame-duck Ford administration, forcing President-elect Jimmy Carter to confront the issue.

The decision to retain or abandon the B-1 project would rest on a number of factors, none of which were firm. While the B-1 was flying, its critical electronic warfare (EW) system had started some four years behind the aircraft itself and would not be tested for some

With ALCM for a partner, the B-52 returned for yet another final comeback performance. Equipped with new avionics to provide the missile's guidance system with an accurate *starting point, this B-52G carries a dozen ALCMs on the pylons originally provided for Hound Dog and Skybolt. The B-52H can now carry eight more ALCMs internally. Boeing*

time; its effectiveness against the known threat, let alone the future threat, was a matter of estimates rather than hard data. The cruise missile was radical and completely new, and had only just started development; unforeseen flaws could lurk behind the attractive numbers. There were many force options to be considered: cruise missiles, plus a reduced B-1 force; B-52s with cruise missiles, to be followed by modified transports carrying dozens of them. Finally, Stealth was on the horizon; while a Stealth bomber could not yet be a credible substitute for the B-1, production of the full 240 B-1s would preclude such a development for generations.

In mid-June of 1977, President Carter took the B-1 question to Camp David. Listing forty-seven arguments for and against on a legal pad, and weighting them with one to five points, he decided to cancel the production program. Partly as a sop to the bomber's supporters, and partly as an insurance policy against changes in the threat or problems with the cruise missile, tests of the B-1 and its EW system would continue. However, most of the B-1 money would be shifted into full-scale development of the cruise missile and a new navigation system for the B-52G/H bombers which would carry it.

These tests included a long series of "bomber penetrativity evaluation" tests, conducted at Nellis AFB in 1979. They produced some remarkable results. At 600 mph, 250 feet above the ground, following a winding track around and over the Nevada mountains, and firing powerful and accurately directed packages of electronic half-truths at any radar close enough to be a problem, the B-1 proved very hard to track. The control centers frequently had no idea where the intruder was until it popped over the hills on its final attack run. The tests were a big step forward for the manned bomber's advocates, and strengthened the will of those in the industry and the services who refused to believe that the bomber would die with the B-52.

... But misses

Meanwhile, engineers and strategic analysts studied a whole range of new weapon systems. Even the USAF's experimental short-runway transport, the AMST, was studied as a cruise-missile carrier; the idea was that it could use any one of thousands of small airfields in a crisis. Rockwell studied dozens of versions of the B-1, with modifications to reduce its cost and to make it more adaptable to other missions, such as conventional bombing or long-range anti-shipping strikes. General Dynamics developed a novel proposal: to take SAC's FB-111As, together with some of Tactical Air Command's F-111s, and to modify them radically, adding the B-1's F101 engine and a new landing gear.

The most radical new bomber proposals resulted from a program called Saber Penetrator. This study assumed that the B-52 or another aircraft would be used to carry cruise missiles, perform Vietnam-type heavy bombing missions or launch anti-shipping missiles, and called for an all-new bomber designed specifically to penetrate Soviet airspace; it was to use the most advanced technology in prospect, and need not be in service before 1990. Not surprisingly, the resulting proposals combined advanced aerodynamics, new materials and, above all, Stealth.

By 1979, only two years after the B-1 had been canceled, SAC commander General Richard H. Ellis no longer regarded its resurrection as a high priority. SAC's preferred "road map" for its bomber force was to continue the B-52-plus-cruise-missile program and, as quickly as possible, to develop the enlarged F-111 and modify 155 aircraft, while launching a long, careful program to develop a Stealth bomber for the nineties.

However, the SAC plan was not backed by the higher echelons of the Air Force command, where the B-1 still enjoyed considerable support. The opinions of the user community, moreover, counted for little among the pro-B-1 politicians, for whom the Rockwell bomber had become a symbol of the "soft on defense" Carter administration. These politicians included presidential candidate (and Californian) Ronald Reagan.

Like Carter before him, Reagan found that the bomber was the first big military-technical decision facing his administration. Having vocally criticized the decision to cancel B-1 production, the new team was committed to launching a new bomber program.

There was still a difference of opinion between SAC and the USAF headquarters on the best approach to take to the requirement. Both shared the view that the Stealth bomber was the best long-term choice for the penetrator role, but that the B-52H, SAC's best in-service penetrating bomber, would be outclassed by Soviet defenses before the new aircraft could be ready. However, while SAC considered that 155 FB-111Hs were equal to 100 B-1s, the USAF command decided to ask for both a resur-

The Soviet Union copied the ALCM concept with the AS-15 Kent cruise missile, which became operational in 1986. The carrier aircraft was the Tupolev Tu-95 Bear-H, a new production model of a bomber contemporary with the B-52. US Department of Defense

rected B-1, incorporating some Stealth technology, and a Stealth bomber.

Northrop alternative

The merits of the rival proposals were debated at length during 1981, with Rockwell promising a reduced, fixed price for the B-1, and the proponents of the Stealth bomber promising better performance and early delivery dates. It was known that Secretary of Defense Caspar Weinberger was unconvinced of the need to develop two new bombers; significantly, the B-1 contractors began to hedge their bets. Rockwell agreed to join Lockheed on its Stealth bomber proposal, while its main associate contractors, Boeing and Vought, decided to join forces with Northrop Corporation.

Lockheed had built the XST prototypes and was producing the operational F-117A, and Rockwell had produced the last two US strategic bombers, but what of Northrop? Before the summer of 1981, anyone who had suggested that Northrop could make a serious run for prime-contractor status on the next strategic bomber would have been quietly removed from the scene and tested for use of controlled substances. The only manned aircraft that Northrop had built in numbers for years was the F-5, a lightweight fighter produced almost entirely for export to allies which could not afford the bigger and more potent machines that the USAF used. Northrop had not built a combat aircraft for front-line USAF service since 1958.

But there was more to Northrop than met the eye. Run by a core group of highly experienced, long-serving engineers and managers, the company had a reputation for advanced thinking. Its

chairman and chief executive officer, Thomas V. Jones (who had been president or chairman since 1959), had helped to originate the concept of "life cycle cost" (LCC) at Northrop in the fifties. By estimating the complete cost of flying and maintaining a fleet of aircraft throughout its active life, LCC analysis showed whether a given design change would cost more or less in the long run.

One of Northrop's leading designers, Lee Begin, had been designing highly agile fighters in the mid-sixties, before the USAF realized how badly it needed them. (Begin's design eventually entered service as the F-18 Hornet.) The company was less reluctant than most aerospace companies to build and equip new plants or to invest its own money in promising ideas; the most conspicuous example was its F-20, the only US fighter since the fifties to be built with private money. (The last private-venture fighter before that had been the first F-5.) Northrop had also grown, through acquisitions and internal development, into an unusually broad-based military aerospace company, with divisions producing advanced navigation systems, ECM equipment and unmanned aircraft.

And, in the mid-sixties, Northrop began to concentrate on Stealth, researching shapes and materials and commissioning the test facilities that the new discipline required. "As a company, we set a course a long time ago, and we stuck to it," chairman Jones remarked at the company's 1988 annual meeting. "We agreed that Northrop would concentrate on fundamental technologies which, if we were successful, would someday—years later, perhaps—be essential for our customers' and our country's success." Important advances were achieved, according to the company's 1988 annual report. "The essential breakthrough by Northrop engineers and scientists involved the ability to design low observability into combat aircraft without compromising aircraft capability," Jones stated. In the mid-seventies, Northrop began hiring more engineers with experience in low observables, reportedly for its own "skunk works" in the Palos Verdes hills.

The other members of Northrop's Stealth bomber team brought their own strengths to the party. Boeing Military Airplane Company knew large aircraft and large programs, and had developed the "offensive avionics system" for the B-1, ensuring that the radar, navigation devices and computers would work together and enable the aircraft to drop bombs accurately. Vought was unusual in that it had deliberately withdrawn from developing and building new aircraft in favor of improving its abilities as a subcontractor to other companies. It was already investing heavily in new technologies such as computer-aided

The B-1B is a large aircraft with three weapon bays designed to accommodate SRAMs or gravity weapons. Compared with the B-1A, the engine inlets have been completely changed to reduce reflectivity. In the process, however, the aircraft has been rendered subsonic for all practical purposes. Rockwell

manufacturing of composite materials, and industrial robotics.

The debate heats up again

Reagan announced the administration's bomber decision on October 20, 1981. It pleased everyone except those who were concerned about whether the Pentagon and the Administration had a firm grasp on financial reality. Production of 100 B-1Bs would start immediately; it would be a fast-paced effort, with the first new bomber to be delivered in 1984 and the last in 1988. The B-1B would start to replace the B-52H in the penetrator mission by 1986, and the B-52s would, in turn, be converted to launch cruise missiles.

Northrop's team was awarded the $7,300 million contract to develop and produce 132 of what was called the Advanced Technology Bomber (ATB)—the official designation B-2 was adopted some time later, but was not publicly used until late 1987. Entering service in the nineties, the B-2 would replace the B-1B as a penetrator, and the B-1Bs would be reassigned as cruise-missile launchers.

It was the most expensive way of acquiring 240 new bombers that had been proposed. It is far cheaper to build 240 aircraft of one type than to split the same total among two different aircraft, each requiring a massive non-recurring investment. There were a number of reasons for the two-bomber program. Some were good, some were questionable and some were merely political. The worst, unquestionably, was that candidate Reagan had savagely criticized Carter's cancellation of the B-1A, had promised to resurrect it and intended to keep

that promise, despite the doubts of some key advisers.

The Air Force could hardly have overlooked political considerations. The year 1984 would bring another presidential election, and, possibly, another Democratic administration. The last two times that the Democrats had won the White House from the Republicans, in 1960 and 1976, the Air Force's new bomber had been dead within a year. The B-2, in the middle of a long development process, would be ripe for the same treatment, but the B-1B would be so far along in production that it would be much harder to kill. For the USAF, nearly thirty years after it had started writing specifications for a B-52 replacement, the B-1 was a bird in the hand.

Publicly, the Air Force and the Pentagon argued that improving Soviet air defenses would render the B-52H incapable of penetrating to its targets by the mid-to-late eighties, before the Stealth bomber could be ready; an "interim penetrator" was therefore required urgently. By the early-to-mid-nineties, however, improving defenses would negate the interim aircraft. The B-1B was depicted as the logical solution since, unlike the improved FB-111, it could be adapted to other heavy bomber missions once its career as a penetrator was over.

The flaw in this argument was that it assumed an ability to predict Soviet developments and deployments, and to assess their effectiveness, over the following fifteen years, against a system which had not yet been fully tested, and to do so with an unrealistic degree of accuracy and confidence. If the Soviet answer to the AWACS, a crucial element

Wing/body blending was applied to the B-1 to reduce weight and RCS. Combined with its *sharply swept wings and use of RAM, it does help the aircraft avoid detection.* Rockwell

in defense against low-flying bombers, turned out to be a poorer performer than expected, or if the new Soviet fighters joined the squadrons later or less quickly than the CIA had guessed, the B-52 could be an effective penetrator for most of the eighties. On the other side of the balance, problems with the B-1 could reduce its margin of superiority over the B-52.

The potential of the B-52 was also underestimated. The B-52's bombing accuracy was being dramatically increased by the cruise-missile-related modification program, and, under a quick-reaction effort called PAVE MINT, its EW systems were being improved. But Reagan had made great play of the age and alleged decrepitude of the B-52 during his election campaign, even though structural surveys showed that the tough old birds could fly well into the twenty-first century, and talking about the B-52 upgrades during 1981 was discouraged.

Had everything gone as planned or predicted, the two-bomber program could have been a success, but the argument for the B-1 as an interim penetrator rested on too many far-reaching projections, many of them inaccurate. The new Soviet fighters appeared several years late; so did the Soviet AWACS, and it turned out to be a poor performer. Above all, the task of developing the B-1's defensive avionics, designed to detect, classify and jam hostile radar, had been disastrously underestimated. By late 1988, the system was inching toward the performance that the USAF originally required. By the time the B-1 is up to standard, the Stealth bomber should be ready to assume the penetrator role.

Development continues

This is not a book about the B-1, but the fortunes of the Rockwell bomber since 1981 have made headlines, worn to a thread the public's tolerance for the bomber lobby and its contractors, and created a much harsher climate for the Stealth bomber. This is a double burden, since Northrop and its partners had committed themselves to a project which involved as many advances as any other aircraft in the history of aerospace.

One of the few factors on the side of the contractors was the fact that the schedule was relatively relaxed. The bomber modernization plan was designed so that it would not cost a wildly unrealistic amount in any given year. Spending on the B-1 would increase very quickly from 1982 to 1985; after that, it would stabilize and decline as some parts of the B-1 production line (making components that were needed years before the aircraft were delivered) began

to shut down. While B-1B spending was at its highest, Northrop and its partners would complete the design of the new bomber, and only then make large-scale preparations for production.

The development schedule was and remains classified, but it was reported at the time the program started that the new bomber was to make its first flight in December 1987, and that it would be operational by the early nineties, probably 1991-92. With the B-1 in hand, however, the USAF was prepared to use the timetable as a tool, rather than letting the schedule drive the program. Instead of pouring money on a problem, or forging ahead with the program, hoping that a solution would be found and that it would not require major rework, the USAF was prepared to let the schedule

B-1 development aircraft in its element: low-altitude, high-speed penetration. Swing wings, considered almost essential for this role, are a major contributor to the bomber's weight and complexity. Rockwell

75

---

slip if a better aircraft could be obtained at lower risk.

Indeed, one role in which the B-1 has been useful (although at considerable cost) is as a back-up to the B-2. Although Lockheed and Northrop thought otherwise, the Pentagon regarded the development of a Stealth strategic bomber as a risky venture in 1981. It seems, from such evidence as Northrop's earnings and the tone of some public statements, that the first thirty-six to forty months of the B-2 program were spent in "risk reduction" efforts, aimed at identifying solutions to some of the more difficult problems posed by the design before the Pentagon committed itself to the huge investment required for production and full-scale development.

If, by early 1985, the B-2 had proved to be less capable or far more expensive than anticipated, the USAF would have had the option of changing requirements or extending the schedule, while buying more B-1s if necessary. To look at the same situation from another angle, the existence of the B-1 would allow the USAF to push for the most advanced B-2 possible, without worrying as much about the schedule as it would have to do if there was no modern bomber in the force.

Black programs

Another reason that the USAF was able to accept delays on the B-2 program, was that such a decision would not produce banner headlines as it would in the case of most other projects. This was because the entire program was secret. From the start of the project, until early 1988, unclassified informa-

tion on the B-2 program amounted to a few dozen words. Northrop, Boeing, Vought and General Electric could be identified as the main contractors, 132 aircraft were to be built, and the bomber was described as incorporating low-observable technology. That was all that the USAF was prepared to say.

At no time in recent history has the Pentagon told the US public about all its projects. Security restrictions reach far beyond plans, communications and technical details. The existence of entire programs is classified; whole classes of equipment are classified, so that any new system in that category is automatically secret. Devices and systems for spying on potential adversaries, for example, are secret. As a result, any new technology applicable to strategic reconnaissance is secret by definition.

Classification levels

Sometimes, these programs are later declassified, or their classification level is reduced. For example, General Electric was cleared in the mid-eighties to discuss the devices that it developed to return film from orbiting spy satellites, because the devices were militarily obsolete and the company wanted to use them as platforms for commercial zero-gravity experiments. In 1982—ten years after the program was terminated—the USAF released photographs of the Lockheed D-21 supersonic reconnaissance drone. Its performance remains secret.

But classification tends to be a one-way trapdoor. It is difficult to declassify anything without proving beyond a reasonable doubt that its disclosure can do no harm. But once something has been secret for a long time, the people who know all the reasons why it was secret have moved on to other jobs or retired, and those who were most senior at the time may even be dead. The quick answer is to lock the documents in a vault and forget about them.

Incredible as it may seem in an open society, the quicksands of classification have engulfed entire airplanes. One highly sensitive experimental airplane, which had been damaged in an accident and was no longer required, was broken up and buried to save the expense of keeping it covered and under guard for an indefinite number of years.

Such projects are generically and unofficially called "black programs." There are different degrees of blackness. The B-2 was not as black as some; its existence was acknowledged and some information was released from the outset. What made the B-2 project different was its sheer size, and the number of companies involved in it. Northrop's first security measure was to remove the project from the rest of the organization, forming a separate division called Advanced Products, and acquiring a closed-down automobile plant at Pico Rivera, California, to house it. The plant was quickly surrounded by fences topped with coiled wire, bristling with razorlike blades.

Security measures at Pico Rivera and other plants have been described as paranoid. But, as the proverb has it, "being paranoid doesn't mean that they're not out to get you." Before the B-2 contract was awarded, a Polish intelligence officer recruited an engineer at Hughes Radar Systems Group, William Bell, and obtained details of the company's work on "quiet" radar systems. Bell was sentenced to eight years in prison in 1981.

There was no way to guarantee that other employees might have been approached and turned by foreign agents. Instead, security measures within the razor-wire perimeter were designed to minimize the damage any one spy could cause.

Compartmentalization

What black programs have in common is that information is controlled by Special Access security regulations. A Special Access clearance is based on the "need-to-know," regardless of level. Information within a Special Access program is "compartmentalized." People working in one area know no more than they need to know about the project as a whole, and those at higher levels are not routinely cleared into all the details of the work which they supervise.

In the late seventies, Boeing studied this all-wing Stealth bomber with tiny ventral rudders and flush inlets. The absence of conventional controls and the straight leading edges foreshadowed the B-2 design. Boeing

Compartmentalization is enforced by means which range from twenty-first-century gadgetry to Biblical simplicity. The latter is typified by the procedures used when a person visits an area where he or she is not cleared into the details of the work (a computer specialist visits an engineering office, for example). The visitor is escorted, a light flashes above the visitor's location, and the escort rings a bell, announcing "Uncleared person in area!"

The high-tech side of security includes secure conference rooms, with double sound-proof doors and motion detectors (so that no agent can plant a bug while the conference room is supposed to be unoccupied). Computers are a necessity but a serious security risk, because they leak electromagnetic signals which can be decoded. (The Pentagon now has a standard for computer

This Boeing study represents a more conservative approach, with a conventional fuselage and separate tail surfaces. The V-tail is remarkably reminiscent of the F-117. Boeing

security, called Tempest, but this had not been defined when the B-2 program started.) Any computers handling sensitive information are housed in metal-lined rooms, also equipped with double doors. Employees and visitors are forbidden to carry personal microcassette recorders and even, in some cases, pocket calculators.

Literal compartmentalization is carried to its extreme in large facilities which are shared by several black programs. One of these is the new radar-cross-section laboratory commissioned by Boeing in early 1988. Designed to plot the radar image of large-scale models (up to half the size of a real fighter) the laboratory's working chamber is two thirds as long as, and a bit wider than, a football field; eighty feet high; lined with radar-absorbent plastic pyramids; and equipped with cable and pylon systems which can position a target with an accuracy of four thousandths of a degree.

Security

Within the building is a complex of chambers where models can be prepared for test and test data can be analyzed. This area is not only secured against outside intrusion, but it is also laid out so that several Special Access programs can use the facility concurrently, while maintaining rigid security barriers between the programs. Models can be prepared for test or modified in secure vaults with eight-inch steel walls, connected by an elevator which is controlled from inside the vaults. All individual control and data-processing rooms are fitted with programmable combination locks and sealed to DoD Tempest standards against electronic leaks. Even the heating and air-conditioning ducts are fitted with steel blocker bars and motion sensors to prevent inter-program intrusion. Before the building was commissioned, Air Force security officials asked Boeing to change a door which opened onto part of the roof. It would be too easy, they said, for an intruder to drop from a helicopter and break in through the door.

The three associate contractors on the B-2 who were identified by the USAF were not permitted to divulge their roles on the program. Other companies were not even named, but the subcontractor list included hundreds of large and small concerns across the United States.

The Southern California aerospace industry is dominated by giants such as Northrop and Lockheed, but it also relies on small job shops producing electronic or structural components to order, in lots which might be uneconomical for a large company. In some cases, Northrop set up cover companies so that these small subcontractors which do not have the facilities to support high security work would not be aware that their components were destined for Pico Rivera.

Black budgets

There were many good reasons for concealing the technical details of the B-2 program. The bomber included so many radical features that it presented the Soviet Union with a challenge of unknown magnitude. Its Stealth design, too, meant that its external shape could provide clues to its detectability. In any event, the practice of publishing technical details of new military aircraft long before they were completed was a recent

Another Boeing study of the late seventies emphasized wing-body-nacelle blending, but was otherwise unusually conventional. Aerodynamically, it would have been much more efficient than Boeing's short-span delta proposals. Like the B-2, it represents an attempt to define a shape which would be Stealthy and yet efficient. Boeing

innovation. In the fifties, the roll-out of a military aircraft was usually the first time that its shape was seen in public, and its weights and performance remained secret long after it entered service. By the seventies, standards had changed so much that the British magazine *Flight International* was able to prepare its phenomenally detailed cutaway drawings of the F-14, F-15 and B-1 while they were still in the flight-test stage.

Classification

The Reagan administration ushered in a global reaction against the liberal security policies of the seventies. Under an executive order signed by Reagan in 1982, Pentagon officials and USAF officers were given new guidelines for classification. National security, not the public's right to know, was to be the primary criterion for determining what should be classified. In case of doubt, officials were to classify a document rather than leave it unclassified, and to classify at a higher rather than a lower level. Senior officials were discouraged from reducing classification levels proposed by people reporting to them.

The effect of this change rapidly spread throughout the military establishment. The expanding Stealth programs, which in another era would have become more accessible as they moved from research into full-scale development, remained black. Indeed, for a time, Pentagon officials and contractors were strongly discouraged from even mentioning the word "Stealth" or "low-observables" in public. However, few people apart from trade and technical reporters were seriously affected by this trend.

What was more controversial was the decision to conceal the costs of the B-2 program from the public. The unclassified versions of annual Pentagon budget requests include sums in the billions of dollars for programs identified only by codenames such as Bernie or Elegant Lady. Further billions are hidden under titles such as "advanced concepts" or "special activities." Both the codenames and the cover phrases change from year to year, so there is no way to track these expenditures individually. The most that can be done is to add up the items in the budget which do not apply to known unclassified programs, to yield an approximate total for the "black budget."

By 1987, one investigation by the *Philadelphia Inquirer* put the black budget at $35 billion, or eleven percent of the total Pentagon budget. The figure

was three times as high as it had been in 1981. About half of it went to support intelligence activities, such as the development of sophisticated reconnaissance satellites, and operations in support of the CIA and National Security Agency. Of the remaining $18 billion for purely military requirements, about $11 billion went for research and development. This total included major systems such as the B-2, the Navy's Advanced Tactical Aircraft and the mysterious "Aurora" reconnaissance aircraft, which appeared in an unclassified budget document in early 1985, probably through a censor's error.

While the detailed breakdown of these totals is secret from the public, the Pentagon maintains that democratic process has not been circumvented, because expenses are still overseen by Congress. The members of the House and Senate Armed Services Committees have special security clearances which give them access to the uncensored Pentagon budgets. However, anything that they learn during closed session cannot be repeated in an open debate, and they appear to have limited influence on the Pentagon when it comes to deciding what should or should not be classified.

In early October 1988, for example, it was widely reported that the USAF was about to reveal the existence of the F-117 Stealth fighter. By October 2, an announcement seemed imminent. According to the *Los Angeles Times*, Defense Secretary Frank Carlucci was prepared to let the cat out of the bag, but was ambushed by Democrats Sam Nunn and Les Aspin (chairmen, respectively, of the Senate and House Armed Services Committees). The Democratic leaders insisted that, since Congress had cooperated with the USAF in keeping the program black, Congress should have some influence on whether it should be declassified. They were partially successful; the Pentagon delayed the announcement until two days after the Presidential election.

Wall Street may be more influential than Congress in limiting the scope of black budgets. In the case of Northrop, analysts have been concerned that the B-2 represents an enormous flow of money through Northrop, relative to its size. The health of the program is key to the health of Northrop, and to Northrop's credit rating.

The Air Force argues that the flow of money into a program gives away its size and its timescale to an adversary. But the size of the B-2 program—132 aircraft—has never been secret. While its schedule may have been uncertain, plus or minus two years, in the early stages of the program, it was fairly obvious by 1985 that the earliest service-entry date would be 1992. However, the USAF continued to keep the costs secret until the end of 1988.

Inflation

Meanwhile, the costs increased. One single jump occurred in 1984, when the center-section structure was redesigned to fix a design problem and, at

This Rockwell all-wing design, also dating back to the 1979-80 period, features buried engines and small fins under the trailing edge. Radar arrays are located in the leading edges of the wings, as they are on the B-2.
Rockwell

the same time, to enable the aircraft to penetrate air defenses at low altitudes should the need arise during its long service life. The change cost $1 billion directly, and probably incurred additional costs through the delay which it caused to the rest of the program.

Before December 1988, the only cost figure released by the USAF was a $36.6 billion "program cost" in 1981 dollars. Program cost, in the USAF's terms, includes research, development, testing and evaluation; training equipment, support equipment and initial spare parts; production tooling; and the cost of each aircraft and all their permanently installed components.

For the sake of comparison, it is worth looking at another, unclassified USAF program: the C-17 transport. The C-17 is due to enter service in 1992, and the USAF aims to buy 210 aircraft by the year 2000; neither the timescale nor the production volume is vastly different from those which apply to the B-2. In 1981 dollars, the C-17 should cost $3.5 billion for development and $17 billion for production. But the bulk of the airplane's development has taken place in the late eighties, so in then-year dollars (the sums actually spent year by year) development will cost $5 billion. Production money is spent much later, so it is even more sharply increased by inflation. Then-year production costs are $30.6 billion.

For the C-17, total program costs of $20.6 billion in 1981 dollars translate to $35.6 billion in actual expenditures between now and 2000, when the final aircraft is due to be delivered. The ruthless laws of manufacturing economics dictate that the price will increase further

if the delivery schedule is stretched out, as nearly always happens.

Apart from keeping Wall Street analysts and writers busy on speculation, the classification of the B-2 cost figures undoubtedly kept the aircraft out of the public mind. The seven-year delay, however, has protected the B-2 during the most vulnerable stages in its development, and through its biggest single crisis. Even though the program still carries some risk, Northrop and the USAF should, by now, have a good idea how much development will cost. Further surprises on the cost front should not occur.

Even so, we are talking about a half-billion-dollar bomber. Whether it costs more than its weight in gold (as did the ill-starred B-58 in its own day) is a matter for dispute and depends on your assumptions on costs and the B-2's empty weight. Its cost may determine whether it ever enters service, and it will certainly affect the timetable for its introduction.

New cost figures were released by the US Air Force on December 16, 1988. USAF Secretary Edward C. Aldridge announced that the program cost had increased to $42.5 billion in 1981 dollars, a sixteen percent increase over the original estimate. This translates to $68.1 billion in then-year dollars, or $515.9 million for each of 132 aircraft. Aldridge noted that these numbers were based on a production schedule that would lead to the last aircraft being delivered in mid-1995.

The announcement of the B-2 costs was Secretary Aldridge's last public duty before he resigned to take up a post with McDonnell Douglas. His successor (not named at the time of this writing), will be the one to deal with a growing controversy, inside and outside the Pentagon, over whether the B-2 should be produced in quantity and, if so, how many should be built each year.

The problem is that costs quoted in December 1988 are based on the most efficient possible production plan, where the production rate increases steadily to the maximum rate that the facilities will support. In this case, a rate of twenty-four aircraft per year would have to be reached by 1991 in order to close the line in 1995. The official plan calls for most of these aircraft to be covered by a single, vast multiyear contract (MYC), allowing the economies of scale to be taken to the maximum extent; everything, from engines to fasteners, could be ordered in 100-aircraft lots.

The question is whether the money exists to do this, desirable as it may be from the standpoint of manufacturing economics.

B-2 timetable

The USAF is unlikely to buy more than fourteen B-2s per year, and some sources suggest the number could be as low as ten. The main reason is cost. The USAF has other large and expensive programs under way, including the C-17 and the Advanced Tactical Fighter. Even among strategic programs, the B-2 must share funding with the expensive and apparently troubled AGM-129 Advanced Cruise Missile, modifications to the B-1 and the conversion of B-52s to fill conventional roles. The budget will simply not accommodate high-rate B-2 production. Even if the USAF wants to buy the

aircraft faster, the rate is likely to be forced down by Congress. Before cost figures were revealed, senior lawmakers were quoted in *The Wall Street Journal* as saying the program would have to be delayed.

A gradual introduction of the B-2 also fits into Strategic Air Command's bomber road map. The command's ninety-six B-52Hs are being modified to carry cruise missiles. With a new internal eight-round common strategic rotary launcher (CSRL) in addition to two six-round pylon launchers, the aircraft can carry as many ALCMs or ACMs as the 166 B-52Gs which filled the cruise-missile launch role up to 1988. Most of the B-52Gs are to be converted for conventional strike missions in the nineties.

As the B-2 enters service, the B-1B will be assigned to the cruise-missile mission. However, this transition will not take place for some time; it involves fitting the B-1Bs with the same CSRLs that are now, in late 1988, being fitted to the B-52H.

The first B-2 base will be Whiteman AFB, near Kansas City in Missouri. According to the USAF, it will receive its first aircraft before the end of September 1991. Plans and statements suggest that it will receive a total of thirty-four B-2s, and that there will be two more operational bases for the type. Covered maintenance areas will be provided for each aircraft, to protect their interior details from observation by satellites. Both the new bases, like Whiteman, are likely to be located in the heart of the Midwest. It is no coincidence that this is the only part of the United States which is beyond the range of submarine-launched SS-N-21 cruise missiles launched from deep Atlantic or Pacific waters.

While Whiteman was named two years ago, subsequent B-2 bases had not been identified late in 1988, so it is likely that the second base will be equipped at least two years after the first.

If the USAF buys only ten aircraft per year, it could well be mid-1993 before Whiteman even has half its planned complement of B-2s, the earliest point at which initial operational capability (IOC) could reasonably be declared. The unit would probably not reach its full strength until some time in 1995.

Admiral William Crowe, Chairman of the Joint Chiefs of Staff, told *The Wall Street Journal*, "I'd like it sooner [than 1995], but I live in the real world." The B-2's future is not assured, despite the bipartisan support which it enjoys in Congress. There will almost certainly be another Presidential election between now and IOC. The Pentagon's plans are still based on budgets which increase year by year. Congress is unlikely to approve them, so the gap between pro-

jected and actual authorizations gets wider the further out you look. As production is stretched out, the costs increase. Aldridge stated, for example, that a savings of $3 billion, resulting from the MYC, had been built into the official estimates. Simply adding this amount to the budget, and adjusting for the non-operational prototype aircraft, pushes the unit program cost toward $550 million.

Deferring production of the B-2 (on the grounds, perhaps, that the B-1 can be modified and upgraded to penetrate throughout the nineties) has been described as "a one-shot cure for Air Force funding problems" releasing up to $5 billion annually. The B-2 can be expected to follow the B-58, the B-70 and the B-1 down the gauntlet of political controversy, and its backers must hope that the outcome will be more favorable—perhaps as a result of the extraordinary capability of the aircraft itself. The only way to begin to comprehend how one aircraft can possibly cost so much money is to look, in detail, at what is truly one of the most revolutionary and ambitious military aircraft of all time.

Chapter 4

Under the skin

Any reasonable assumptions will always result in an advantage to the all-wing configuration, of such magnitude as to fully warrant whatever trials and tribulations may be involved in its development.

John K. "Jack" Northrop, 1947

Northrop's B-2 rolled from a hangar at Palmdale for its formal debut just over seven years after the development contract had been signed. It was the first time that the aircraft, or any one of its major components, had been seen by anyone who had not been sworn to secrecy, under penalty of incarceration. The dramatic effect was undeniable, because the B-2 looks like no other vehicle in the history of aviation.

The only airplanes which have ever looked remotely like the B-2 were flown in the forties, when designers in the United States, Britain and Germany were pursuing the idea of an all-wing airplane or Flying Wing. As its name suggests, the all-wing airplane has neither fuselage nor tail, but carries all its payload, fuel and components inside the wing. But even those distant ancestors did not share the single dominating, most bizarre feature of the B-2's shape.

Viewed from directly above or below, the B-2's boomerang-like shape comprises twelve ruler-straight lines. The leading edges, the long sides of the boomerang, run straight from the extreme nose to the extreme tips of the wing. The wingtips are not parallel with the airflow, like those on most normal airplanes, but are cut off at a near-right-angle to the leading edges. Apart from the tips, the outer wings have no taper; again, completely unlike any normal aircraft. The inner trailing edges form a jagged shape, jutting rearward toward the centerline.

Look at the B-2 from any point in the horizontal plane, however, and the shape changes. In front, rear or side view, the bomber has virtually no straight lines and no hard edges. The top and bottom surfaces are both continuous, three-dimensional curved surfaces. Even the over-wing air inlets, which look jagged from a distance, can be seen at close range to be made up of many curved segments. There are even very few curves of constant radius; rather, the surfaces change radius continuously, as though they were produced from segments of a spiral. The shape has no abrupt distinctions between body and wing. A dorsal hump with the cockpit in front rises smoothly from the top surface, but the underside swells gradually from the outermost trailing-edge kink to the centerline.

Combined with the things that the eye expects to see, but which are not there—engine pods, a fuselage, a vertical fin and a stabilizer—the effect is to make the B-2 look like something organic rather than a machine; like an immense manta-ray, improbably resting on its wheels in the high desert of California.

Nothing in aircraft design is accidental, very little is influenced by convention and much less by style. The size and shape of an aircraft is the result of a compromise hammered out between the requirements imposed by the job which the aircraft has to do.

There is a cartoon, not much younger than the airplane itself, that is probably found in every aircraft design office in the world. It shows an aircraft as each group in the team designed it. The aerodynamics group's design is slender, smooth and flowing. The production group's contribution is usually represented by four planks, nailed together in the shape of an airplane. The maintenance group's design is a mass of access panels, with all the control cables and hydraulic pipes on the outside, and so on. The point of the cartoon is that none of the designs is workable in itself.

The different groups have to compromise, or "trade," accepting less-than-optimum in one area in order to meet minimum requirements in another.

Speed, range, payload and what engineers call "-ilities" (reliability, maintainability, supportability) are all part of the "trade studies" which take place in the earliest stages of design. What makes the B-2 look so strange is the simple fact that a completely new and very important "-ility" was added to the trade studies back in 1977-78: observability.

That much said, low-observables technology, or Stealth, differs from other design qualities in a number of important ways. Its benefits are mainly apparent when it is given high priority, so that the aircraft is not just twice as difficult to detect as a conventional type, but ten or a hundred times more so. When it is applied in such a way, Stealth tends to be the main driver behind the design, just as sustained Mach 3 performance was the main driver in the design of the SR-71. Unlike some technologies (such as new materials or electronics) Stealth directly affects the outside shape of the airplane. For these reasons, Stealth aircraft look drastically different from other aircraft.

According to Ben Rich, leader of the Lockheed team which created the F-117, "a Stealth aircraft has to be Stealthy in six disciplines: radar, infrared, visual, acoustic, smoke and contrail. If you don't do that, you flunk the course."

Radar

If that is the case, why do most studies of Stealth concentrate on radar? The answer is that the importance that you assign to each of the six disciplines depends on the threat that you are facing. A ground-hugging military helicopter is likely to be heard before a radar can pick it up, and is more likely to be targeted by an infrared homing weapon than a radar-directed one, so acoustic and thermal signatures are important. A submarine is a perfect example of a system which is Stealthy in the acoustic spectrum, almost exclusively.

Military airplanes, however, face their greatest threat from radar. Radar can pick an airplane up at a greater distance than any other sensor; large airborne or ground-based early-warning radars have an effective range of 200 to 300 miles, and the only reason that they are not built with greater range is that they run into line-of-sight limits against most targets. The range of the best infrared systems (the closest competitor) is in the high tens of miles under ideal conditions. Unlike infrared, radar gives a very precise estimate of the target's position, and can track the changes in a target's position and determine its speed and course, both of which are essential to achieving an interception. Emerging radar technology, using high-speed processors to analyze the return radar signal in ways which would have taken hours of computer time a few years ago, can even find ways to identify the type of aircraft on the screen.

Applied to military aircraft, Stealth means, first, reducing the range at which radar can detect the aircraft and, second, reducing observables in the other five categories to the point where the detection range in those spectra is not significantly greater, whatever combi-nation of available or forecast technologies may be used.

How it works

All radar systems, from an AWACS to a police speed radar, work in the same way. A radio-frequency signal is transmitted through a directional antenna which focuses it into a conical beam. When a reflective target (in radar jargon, anything observed by radar is a target) blocks part of the beam, that part of the beam is reflected in many different directions, or "scattered." If the scattering is fairly random, as is usually the case, some energy will be reflected in the direction of the radar antenna. Most radars transmit energy in pulses, thousands of them every second. In the gaps between the pulses, the radar becomes a receiver, and the gaps are long enough for the signal to make its way to the target and back at the speed of light.

The interval between the transmission and reception of the pulse gives the range from the radar to the target. The radar antenna moves at a regular rate, so the time at which the target moves in and out of the beam can be tied to the position of the antenna, giving the target's bearing from the location of the radar.

This remarkable process has been considerably developed and refined in the half century since the first workable radars were deployed. However, it is still true that radar does not "see" things in the way that the human eye does. We see in a world which is saturated with visible light, so that almost every square inch of it reflects some light toward us at all times; the radar only "sees" the energy that is reflected toward it. The radar can detect a target only when the antenna captures enough energy to rise above the electronic noise that is invariably present in the receiver. All the variables in the transmission-scattering-reflection chain affect the maximum range at which this can happen. These variables include the strength of the signal, the width of the beam, the size of the antenna and the reflectivity, or RCS, of the target.

Target characteristics

The radar beam, it is important to remember, is a cone. The greater the range, the greater the area illuminated by the radar, and the smaller the proportion of the energy which will be scattered by a target of constant RCS. Exactly the same effect results in the scattered energy returning to the radar; at a longer range, the already-reduced energy hitting the target is scattered over a wider area and less of it will be captured by the antenna.

Increasing the power of the radar will increase its range, but the benefits are limited by the fact that much of the extra radiated energy is wasted on empty space. Greater power can also mean more noise in the system. A bigger antenna is helpful, because it can produce a narrower, more intense outgoing beam and intercepts more returned energy. The limit is the size of the antenna, which is important on any mobile or transportable radar and critical on an airborne system.

Target RCS is the one variable that is out of the radar designer's control. The relationship of RCS to the detection range is not in direct proportion, because of the conical beam and radial scatter-

ing effects. Detection range is in proportion to the fourth root of RCS. If a radar has a range of 100 miles against a target with an RCS of 10 square meters, its range will be eighty-five miles against a target of half the reflectivity (5 square meters). A square meter RCS translates into a fifty-five-mile detection range. Thus a ninety percent reduction in reflectivity equals a forty-five percent reduction in detection range; hardly a very inspiring feature.

What makes Stealth possible is that far larger reductions in target RCS are achievable, and the reason that they are achievable is that conventional, un-Stealthy aircraft are almost ideal radar targets. Searching for an aircraft with radar can be compared to searching with a flashlight for a tiny model airplane suspended somewhere in a pitch-black concert hall, hung with matte-black drapes. How hard it will be to find the model depends on many things other than its size. If the model aircraft is white in color, it may be picked out easily. If it is highly polished, it will glint; the observer will see patches of light on its surface that seem almost as bright as the flashlight. The glints will be particularly strong if the model has flat surfaces which are angled at ninety degrees to the source of the light.

Other targets may have completely different characteristics. A flat mirror might seem likely to be highly visible, but unless its surface makes two right angles to the beam (that is to say, it is "normal" to the beam), it will reflect all the light away from an observer. A bowling ball does the opposite; it always reflects the same amount of light, regardless of its attitude.

Light waves are much shorter than radar waves, so most surfaces appear rough to a light wave; energy is scattered randomly by the many tiny pits in the surface. Smoother surfaces (like a polished car body) directly reflect some of the light that strikes them, and a very smooth surface, like a mirror, directly reflects most of the light.

To the radar wave, most synthetic surfaces, like the skin of an aircraft, are mirror-like. A conventional aircraft has a complex external shape, full of curves, flat panels and edges. While its shape agrees with the laws of aerodynamics and the principles of engineering, it is entirely random in terms of the way it scatters radar energy. As the airplane moves (rapidly, relative to a radar which is pulsing energy toward it), it throws off a constantly changing, scintillating pattern of concentrated reflections. The radar designer could ask for little better.

RCS

The measurement called RCS was originally developed by radar engineers. RCS is determined by first measuring, or calculating, the amount of radar energy reflected from a target toward an observer. RCS is based on the size of a

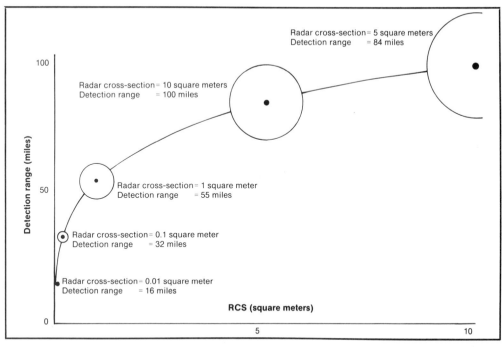

RCS is only one factor determining radar detection range, and the two are not directly proportional. This figure is based on a radar which can detect a 10 square meter target (such as a B-1B) at 100 miles range, and shows its range against smaller targets.

Note that most of the reduction in radar range occurs for targets of 1 square meter RCS (a one-order reduction) or smaller. Where stealth is a primary design objective, RCS will probably be in the region of 0.01-0.1 square meter.

reflective sphere (the optical equivalent would be a spherical mirror) that would return the same amount of energy. The projected area of the sphere, or the area of a disk of the same diameter, is the RCS number itself.

The most important point to be made about RCS is that a small, efficient reflector (such as a flat plate, normal to the radar beam) can reflect as much energy as a very large sphere, and will have a very large RCS. A square plate, 10 cm by 10 cm (3.937 in.), has an area of 0.01 square meter; its RCS, when it is normal to the radar beam, is 1 square meter, or 100 times as large as the actual plate. Composite shapes can be worse. Reflective panels at ninety degrees to one another can turn a radar signal through two right angles and fire it back to the receiver in full intensity.

Many modern aircraft are full of such reflectors, and the resulting RCS figures are almost staggering. Viewed from the side, a typical fighter, such as the F-15 Eagle, may have a projected area of 25 square meters. Because of the aircraft's design, however, the broadside RCS may be sixteen times as large, at 400 square meters, or the size of a very large house. Typical frontal-aspect RCS figures for modern aircraft run around 10 square meters for fighters, and 1,000 square meters for a bomber such as the B-52 or a transport aircraft like the 747.

Minimizing RCS

It follows that the Stealth designer's creed starts with the same words as the physician's Hippocratic oath: "First, do no harm." There are some popular design features which are incompatible with low RCS. Engines in external pods or hung on pylons, such as those of the B-52, provide many excellent retro-reflectors. Vertical stabilizers and slab-sided bodies are ruled out. And external stores (bombs, missiles or fuel tanks) are about as acceptable as facial warts at the Miss America contest.

The Stealth designer can take advantage of the fact that the most threatening radar beams will illuminate his aircraft from a point that is much more distant horizontally than vertically. Most radar waves will impinge on the target from a narrow range of shallow angles. If as much as possible of the surface of the aircraft is highly oblique to those angles, the RCS will be low because most of the energy will be scattered. This can be accomplished by blending the airplane's bulky body into the wing.

Engines produce strong radar reflections and have to be concealed in some way, while permitting air to reach the engine efficiently. However, this tends to demand a long, complex inlet system, which takes up a great deal of internal space. The prohibition on external stores puts further pressure on internal volume.

The Horten brothers realized by 1943 (only five years after the first air-defense radars had been built) that the flying wing met all these basic requirements. It is free of fins and vertical body sides, the main surfaces are highly oblique to the angles from which it is most likely to be illuminated, and the engines are (again, by virtue of the basic design) buried within the wings. Because the main purpose of the flying wing was to achieve lower drag, the Horten aircraft were designed to carry all their fuel and weapons internally.

Jack Northrop, the founder and technical leader of the California company that bore his name, also realized that his flying wings would be less detectable than bombers of conventional configuration. The XB-35 had massive metal propellers which would have confounded any efforts at RCS reduction, but it would have been harder for a fighter pilot to see at cruising height; an important factor when the bomber was designed, because few fighters at that time carried radar. Its jet-powered derivative, the YB-49, was a different case, and Northrop promoted its reduced radar detectability as a significant advantage, carrying out demonstration flights in 1948 against coastal radar stations.

Flying-wing design

Neither Northrop nor the Horten brothers, nor any of the other designers, had developed the flying wing because of its low-observables characteristics. They had pursued the concept because they felt that it was a better way to design airplanes, aerodynamically and structurally. The flying wing's reduced detectability was a serendipitous benefit and a useful selling point.

The reverse case applied when Northrop designers approached the requirement for a new bomber in the late seventies. They had Stealth uppermost in their minds, but the B-2 emerged nonetheless as a flying wing, aerodynamically and structurally closer to the ideal of an all-wing airplane than any aircraft since its ancestor, the Northrop YB-49 of the late forties. The arguments in favor of the all-wing layout have not changed since then; the only difference is that some attributes of the all-wing design,

considered of secondary importance forty years ago, are now critical to achieving Stealth objectives in an efficient design.

Flying wings and their advocates have existed as long as the airplane itself. In Britain, J. W. Dunne flew a tailless aircraft in 1909, and demonstrated that it was inherently stable. It was the German designer Hugo Junkers, however, who appears to have been first to conceive of a true flying wing or "all-wing" aircraft, which would not only have no tail but would have no body. The payload, the crew, the fuel and the engines would be accommodated inside a large, thick wing.

To those who followed in Junkers' tracks, the flying wing seemed to be not only a more efficient class of aircraft, but the only logical shape for almost any type of aircraft.

Lift and drag

The conventional airplane has a wing to lift it and two tail surfaces—a vertical fin and a horizontal tailplane—each with a hinged flap at the back. The fixed tail surfaces keep the aircraft straight and level and the hinged flaps steer it. The airplane's body or fuselage started out as a simple skeletal frame, which supported the tail at a distance from the wing and gave it enough leverage to do its job. Later, the frame was skinned over and used to accommodate the airplane's load.

Both Northrop and the Hortens saw the benefits of flying wings in the same way. The fuselage and tail assembly represented weight and drag. The conventional rear fuselage was particularly heavy, because it had to carry the twisting and bending loads imposed by the

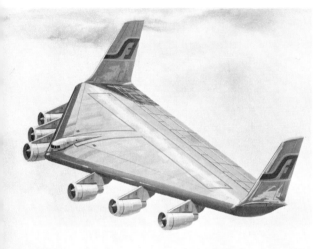

The flying-wing concept was revived in the early seventies, with proposals for massive "spanloader" freighters, some of them designed to carry oil from remote drilling sites. Lockheed

tail surfaces. The fin and tailplane themselves were heavy and added to the surface area of the airplane, but provided neither lift nor useful space. In a conventional aircraft, drag was also caused by aerodynamic interference between the wing and the fuselage, and between the fuselage and tail surfaces.

The flying wing was also structurally efficient. The wing of a conventional aircraft can be compared to a beam with a heavy weight (the body) hung at its mid-point. The wing produces lift along its span—it can be visualized as a line of elastic cables supporting the beam. Clearly, the weight in the middle will bend the beam downward. In a flying wing, however, the mass of the aircraft is spread evenly along the wingspan, so the bending loads are much smaller and the wing can be lighter.

The flying wing, according to Northrop, would have less drag than the conventional aircraft of the same weight, and could cruise faster on less power. It would need less fuel to attain a given range, and could carry more payload. Northrop's XB-35 was designed to carry the same weight of bombs as the Convair B-36, over the same distance, but it would do so at two-thirds the gross weight and two-thirds the power, having four R-4360 engines instead of six. However, the advantages of the flying wing were never decisively demonstrated, first because of engine troubles with the XB-35 and then because the development of the jet-powered YB-49 was terminated after relatively few flying hours. Test results were controversial, with some pilots claiming that the aircraft were unstable and Northrop engineers and pilots asserting that there were no problems which could not be solved with development.

Stability

The truth is that while flying wings do offer considerable improvements in performance, they also present some design challenges, and the tools to solve some of these were not available in the forties. Stability and control were one obvious example. It was a rare airplane in those days that did not undergo some sort of redesign to its tail surfaces during development; to solve a problem in the airplane's handling, designers could make small changes to the size and shape of the fin, rudder or stabilizer. A flying wing is different: its behavior about all three axes tends to be coupled (a movement in yaw tends to result in a movement in pitch) and there are no tail surfaces to provide a quick fix.

The majestic Northrop XB-35 cruises in company with a P-61. The Flying Wing has its split "brudders" (brake/rudders) open-ed, to match its speed with the slower conventional bomber. Northrop

Free of propellers, the YB-49 presented a shape of almost eerie simplicity. The only vertical surfaces were fences and small fixed fins, which prevented unwanted airflow along the span and compensated for the stabilizing effect of the XB-35's propellers. The eight J35 engines were each small enough to be buried inside the wing. Northrop

Looking back, it is amazing that the large and radical XB-35 and YB-49 flew as well as they did, with first-generation power-boosted flight controls (specially developed by Northrop) and no modern electronics. The YB-49 did not meet Air Force handling requirements in that it took too long for the pilot to level out for a bombing run. Late in the test program, however, Northrop fitted the aircraft with a Minneapolis-Honeywell invention, a device that detected and automatically corrected the aircraft's motions in yaw. It was called a stability augmentation system (SAS) and was the forerunner of today's fly-by-wire flight control systems.

High-speed stability was also a problem. Northrop's own X-4, designed to evaluate the high-speed behavior of tail-less aircraft, showed a rapid reduction in stability above Mach 0.88. (Scott Crossfield, one of the pilots who explored the X-4's envelope, later drew his own conclusion from the program, "Airplanes and aviators both need a respectable amount of tail.") Combined with the tendency of all-wing aircraft to accelerate very rapidly in a dive, because of their low drag, this could make pilots nervous at such speeds.

One of the most telling criticisms of the flying wing was the argument that it was better to design the wing purely as a lifting surface rather than compromising it to accommodate the load and provide stability and control. By the late forties, manufacturers such as Boeing were driving toward efficient conventional aircraft with relatively small wings.

The tiny Northrop X-4 revealed high-speed stability problems with tailless aircraft, which played a part in shelving the all-wing *concept until fly-by-wire systems were perfected.* Northrop

Increases in wing loading (aircraft weight divided by wing area) were made possible by the use of large flaps and slats on the leading and trailing edges of the wing. However, a large and effective stabilizer was needed to balance the aircraft when these flaps were used, and to rotate the wing to the high angles of attack where they would be effective. The flying wing, it seemed, could not use such devices, and needed a large, lightly loaded wing, reducing its weight and drag advantage.

It appeared, too, that the move toward higher speeds in the late forties might seal the flying wing's fate. At high speeds just below the speed of sound, supersonic shock waves begin to form above an aircraft's wing, where the air is accelerated by the wing's curvature. At the time, the only way to delay such phenomena to higher speeds (above the relatively slow limits of the YB-35 and YB-49) was to make the wing thinner in section. But this militated against the whole object of the flying-wing design, because it prevented components from being built into the wing.

The flying wing went into a long period of suspended animation after the last of the big Northrop bombers was grounded in 1951. This was partly due to problems with the concept, but was more attributable to the lack of a mission. Jack Northrop himself had noted in 1947 that the benefits of the flying

Low-observables, forties-style: the YB-49 diminished into a pencil-thin line in front view, and its radar signature was certainly lower than that of most contemporary aircraft. Northrop

Low-observables, eighties-style: the B-2 is much deeper than the YB-49, and is probably about 75 percent heavier. The guard in front of the nosewheel puts this very large aircraft in proportion. Bill Sweetman

wing were greatest when the configuration was close to an ideal, with everything inside the wing. This is difficult for a small aircraft such as a fighter, because components of fixed size such as the pilot and the engines cannot be squashed into a wing-shaped envelope. It is also hard to achieve on a cargo aircraft, because its loads are so large that only a vast flying wing can accommodate them without a discrete fuselage. The bomber, a large aircraft with small, dense payloads, is clearly the most suitable candidate for an all-wing approach. The trouble was that, from 1954 onward, SAC wanted supersonic bombers, or bombers that could fly fast at low level. Until, that is, the first ideas of a Stealth bomber took shape in 1977.

Fly-by-wire

While the flying wing had been dormant, advances in the state of the art had provided potential solutions to many of its problems. Stability and control were an example. From the early SAS tested on the YB-49 had stemmed a line of more sophisticated devices, designed to tame the behavior of supersonic aircraft by sensing and counteracting any divergence before it could endanger the aircraft, and before the average pilot could sense it and react. The A-12, ancestor of the SR-71 Blackbird, was the first aircraft which was not safely flyable without its "stab-aug" operating, and was thus the first to have a multiplex, redundant system.

As electronic components became smaller and more reliable, designers realized that the redundant stab-aug system could be mated with another new technology: the use of electronic signals, rather than steel cables or rods, to control the hydraulic actuators which move the airplane's control surfaces. The advantage of this system, called "fly-by-wire" or FBW, was that it was very responsive; unlike a mechanically signaled system, it could adjust the controls many times per second. Unlike the earlier stab-aug systems, it could stabilize an aircraft during a dynamic maneuver rather than limiting its excursions from a constant flightpath.

Stability

The next step was the realization that an aircraft with a reliable fly-by-wire system need not be naturally stable. This technology was first applied to fighters such as the F-16 and F-18, making them lighter and more maneuverable. It is used on the Airbus A320 airliner, allowing it to get by with a smaller, lighter tail and reducing drag.

For the B-2, however, the importance of FBW and artificial stability is not just that it has made it possible to eliminate even the tiny fixed fins of the B-49, although that is a major advantage in terms of low observables. It is also of tremendous help in solving the old problem of low wing loading and a consequently oversized wing. What is truly astonishing is that Jack Northrop knew this in 1947.

Northrop's idea was to place the airplane's center of gravity behind the wing's center of lift. The flying wing would want to pitch upward, but it could be balanced at high speeds by a small downward deflection of the trailing edge (or greater lift on the outer, aft sections of the wing), and at low speeds by deflecting the high-lift flaps which the flying wing otherwise could not use.

The obvious problem would be that the aircraft would be unflyable—unless, Northrop noted, "highly reliable automatic pilots . . . take over the function of stability." Northrop was probably right when he described this idea as "possibly a bit horrifying" in 1947, but it has become an essential feature of the B-2.

FBW has yet another benefit for the flying wing. Because the system is so responsive, it can cause the controls to react as soon as the aircraft hits an air gust. Rather than absorbing the shocks imposed by rough air in its structure, the aircraft actively resists it through the control system. The aircraft can be lighter since the structure does not have to be as strong, and it will ride more smoothly, particularly at low level.

Time has also dealt with the transonic problem. In the forties, aerodynamicists designing transonic wings estimated pressures and velocities with mechanical calculators and slide rules. In the sixties, computers made it possible to develop better mathematical models of the flows over the wing. In the seventies, it became possible to model these flows in three dimensions, instead of treating them as a series of slices. The high-subsonic-speed wings of jet airliners changed visibly from one generation to the next. They became deeper at the tips, changed section and were twisted to a much greater extent along the span, and became very much thicker at the root. The new wings had lower drag, were lighter and could store more

Electronically signaled flight controls (fly-by-wire), driven by high-speed digital computers, have made it possible to fly highly unstable aircraft such as the Grumman X-29, with its forward-swept wing. Similar controls are used on the B-2. Grumman

Northrop proposed this fighter jointly with Germany's Dornier company to meet the Luftwaffe's TKF90 advanced fighter requirement. It is interesting in that it represented an early study in the use of thrust vectoring for control. Northrop

fuel than the wings of the earlier generation of aircraft.

Return of the Wing

The aircraft which emerged from the Palmdale hangar in November 1988, therefore, is not just a revival of the flying wing, but a new interpretation of the concept in the light of current aviation technology.

One of the most important features of the B-2's shape is the way that the serrations of the trailing edge build up to a point in the center, well behind the line formed by the outboard trailing edges. At close range, it is also apparent that the line of maximum depth in the wing takes a rearward bend on the inboard section, curving toward the tail, and the shape is far more three-dimensional, reflecting recent aerodynamic developments, than the flat shape of the YB-49. The center section is also deep,

In April 1988, the USAF released the first artist's impression of the new B-2. It was more accurate than most people thought, *although the over-wing exhausts were omitted.* USAF

much deeper than anyone had expected. In front view, the B-2's underbelly curves downward from the mid-span point to the centerline; from some angles, it resembles a manta-ray in an advanced stage of pregnancy. The result is that the B-2 is bigger and heavier than it looks at first sight. It also carries a great deal of weight aft of the center of lift, and is—as Jack Northrop proposed in 1947—naturally unstable.

Controls

The General Electric digital flight control system (DFCS) is, in consequence, one of the most critical subsystems on the aircraft. This is almost certainly a quadruplex system with four separate channels. Even after a failure in one channel, three channels remain operational. If a second channel starts to fail, the system's logic will detect that it is functioning differently from the two healthy channels and shut it down. The system is certainly not mechanically signaled; the only question is whether its commands are carried to the control actuators by electronics, or by light signals carried by fiber-optic strands. "Fly-by-light," as the latter system is known, operates in precisely the same way as FBW, but is more resistant to electromagnetic pulse (EMP) interference of the kind produced by nuclear explosions. A fly-by-light system might be light-

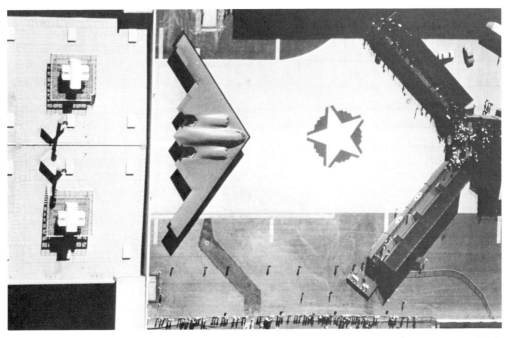

From above, the B-2's overwing exhausts are clearly visible, as are what appear to be movable flaps behind them. Large, plain trailing-edge flaps are fitted along most of the span, and radar-absorbent material is applied along the leading-edge and wingtips. Aviation Week

er and less complex than an FBW system for the B-2, because it would need much less shielding.

The DFCS controls eight large, simple flaps which comprise most of the B-2's trailing edge. Because the B-2's center of gravity is set well aft, these devices can be used to increase lift on take-off and landing. Moreover, the deep kinks in the trailing edge of the wing place the B-2's large flaps well forward, not far behind the center of gravity. They can therefore be deflected quite sharply without unbalancing the aircraft.

Also under the control of the DFCS are two pairs of smaller flaps, located directly behind the overwing exhausts. What makes these surfaces unique is that, when they move, they change the engine thrust vector; if they are moved upward, they deflect the efflux directly, and if they are inclined down, they turn the exhaust through the Coanda effect, the phenomenon that causes water to flow down the outside of a wineglass. The B-2 is the first aircraft to use thrust vectoring for flight control.

External shape

Precisely how all the surfaces work together in order to increase lift at low speeds, damp out gusts and stabilize and steer the aircraft is not clear. However, it is probable that thrust vectoring plays its most important role at low airspeeds, where conventional aerodynamic controls are least effective. Located well aft of the aerodynamic center, the vectoring nozzles would provide effective and responsive pitch control, up to and beyond the stall. Differential vectoring of the left and right engine

pairs could be used for roll control. Moreover, the design of the vectoring flaps is such that they could generate a strong yawing moment if the flaps in each pair were moved differentially.

The overall shape which Northrop has chosen for the B-2 makes sense both aerodynamically and structurally. It allows the flying wing to develop high lift, and provides room in the center section for all the bulky items the bomber must hold. But the details of the shape which make the B-2 look so strange—the rectilinear plan-view and the curvaceous elevations—have little to do with aerodynamics and a great deal to do with Stealth, particularly in the radar spectrum.

Flat surfaces

There are two ways of using geometry to control the way a body scatters a radar wave, and the B-2 uses them both. One is to make the shape flat or rectilinear. This concentrates the reflection on one bearing, and the body can then be constructed so that that reflection will never go toward the likely location of a receiver. This is the principle behind the "faceted" F-117A. Any radar which illuminates the F-117 "sees" a small number of flat surfaces. The radar energy, instead of being scattered at random, is reflected in mirror-fashion from these surfaces.

Unless the radar beam makes two ninety-degree angles to one of the surfaces (which is unlikely, except at extreme look-down angles), it will see virtually nothing. This philosophy seems to be used to control the reflections from the edges of the B-2's airframe. A radar which illuminates the B-2 from anywhere in the front quadrant would produce only two strong "glint" reflections, one from each wing. The probability that one of these reflections will be detected is thus minimal. The trailing edge is likewise composed of a minimum number of straight lines. Ideally, from the RCS standpoint, one might want an aircraft of diamond planform, but the B-2 design represents a compromise between Stealth and aerodynamic efficiency.

Curved surfaces

The second way of shaping a low-RCS body seems almost diametrically opposed to the first. When Stealth was first discussed, the tendency was to assume that Stealth aircraft would have curved exteriors. This, however, is only half right. A constant curve is an isotropic scatterer. It reflects equally in all directions, an effect which has been likened to the rear window of a Volkswagen Bug, gleaming in the sun.

The B-2's curves constantly change radius, as though they are sections of a spiral rather than arcs of a circle. Looking at the B-2, it is hard to avoid the impression that an arcane geometrical theory is at work; that each individual curve, from the large radii of the windshield to the contours of the inlets, is an expression of a single set of laws.

That is simple enough to say. In fact, the process of designing an aircraft so that its exterior shape is in complete accordance with the principles of electromagnetic scattering as well as the laws of aerodynamics is almost unbelievably complex. And it probably could not have been attempted before the advent of supercomputers.

Internal volume

As noted above, the B-2 has more internal volume than most people ex-

pected. Structurally, the aircraft seems to comprise the untapered outer wings, extending from the outermost trailing-edge kink to the tips, and a very deep, ninety-foot-span torsion box. Inside this box are the two weapon bays, the engines and the main landing gear, surrounded by a vast amount of fuel.

The USAF has said that a force of 120 B-2s would be able to deliver approximately 2,000 nuclear weapons, or sixteen per aircraft. Boeing has developed an Advanced Applications Rotary Launcher (AARL) for the B-2. Rotary

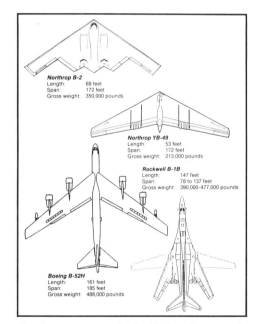

Bombers compared: the B-2's wingspan is identical to that of the YB-49. Its weight, however, is much greater, and it can probably carry as many weapons as far as the much larger and heavier B-52H. The B-1B's variable-sweep wing is much smaller in relation to the airplane's weight than the wings of the B-2 or B-52H; at maximum weight, the B-2 will be a much better-performing aircraft.

launchers have been used on US bombers since the mid-sixties; the weapons are attached to a central tube which carries all the necessary umbilical connections and an ejection system for each store. Presumably, the B-2 carries two eight-round launchers, designed to carry the Boeing AGM-131 SRAM II missile or the B83 gravity bomb.

Cockpit hump

From the first artist's impression of the B-2, it seemed obvious that the cen-

A B-52C shows off features that offset some of the theoretical advantages of the all-wing airplane. Huge Fowler-type flaps increase both the camber and the area of the wing, but cannot be used in an aircraft without a horizontal stabilizer. Engines and fuel tanks are spread along the wingspan, providing some "span-loading" and reducing the bending force on the wing spars. Boeing

Oversize cabin windows deceive the eye, making the B-2 look much smaller than it really is. The windows are large because they are a long way from the pilots' seats.

Note the position of the ejection-seat hatches. The jagged shape of the nose-wheel door breaks up any strong reflections from the gap around the door. Bill Sweetman

tral hummock behind the cockpit contained the weapon bay. However, it seems from more recent views that the weapon load could be contained inside the wing itself. So why is the hump there at all? Another puzzling aspect of this feature is that it is considerably wider than it would have to be if it were simply a fairing behind the cockpit. The B-2's cockpit windows are huge, so large that they throw the aircraft out of proportion and make it look smaller than it is. They are large for the same reason that the cockpit windows of a DC-10 are large; a cockpit window has to provide the pilot with a given angular field of view, and the farther the window is from the pilot's seat, the bigger it has to be. Comparing the location of the ejection-seat hatches with the width of the dorsal hump shows how wide and high the latter is. A possible explanation is that the hump contains much of the B-2's avionics.

Avionics are gregarious; it is most convenient to install them together, so that they can share power supplies and cooling air. On the other hand, the maintenance people prefer to be able to remove any given electronic unit without pulling six others in the process. In a conventional aircraft, the avionics racks occupy much of the forward fuselage, which is skinned with access panels so that everything can be reached and removed.

Where would they be put in a flying wing? If they were placed inside the wing, they could not be reached except from above or below, which would make simple, secure racking a virtual impossibility. Northrop may have elected to provide a dorsal hump in the interests of maintainability.

The engines, outboard of the weapon bays, are also buried completely within the wing. The raised structures behind the inlets, which looked like engine nacelles in the first USAF impression, are simply fairings. The engines can presumably be reached and removed from below for maintenance.

Engine

The B-2 is powered by four General Electric F118-GE-100 engines. The F118 is a member of a phenomenally successful family which includes the B-1's F101 engine, the F110 fighter engine which powers some F-16s and the latest F-14s, and the CFM56, the world's best-selling commercial engine. The F118 is, basically, an F110 without an afterburner.

Here is another puzzle. The F110 was developed from the B-1 engine, the F101, by fitting a smaller low-pressure spool and thereby reducing the bypass ratio from 2:1 to 0.87:1. The result was a slightly slimmer and lighter engine which would fit in a fighter, but which would use more fuel at subsonic speed. Why choose a fighter engine for the B-2 when a more efficient engine was not only available but was in service with Strategic Air Command?

The answer, probably, is that the biggest problem in propulsion for a Stealth aircraft is the design of the inlets, which have to conceal the highly visible first stage of the engine from radar while supplying it efficiently with air. The F101 is a more efficient engine, considered in isolation, but it needs more air than the F110 and its larger fan is a bigger radar target. It would there-

The slit-like secondary inlet, below the main opening, scoops away "boundary layer" airflow which has become turbulent due to skin friction. Otherwise, the turbulence would propagate in the inlet duct and could cause engine-handling difficulties. RAM is visible inside the sharply bent S-shaped duct which leads to the engines. Bill Sweetman

The extraordinary shape of the B-2 inlet resembles something from the crypt of a Gothic cathedral more than part of an airplane. As with the rest of the aircraft, the shape is intended to break up incoming radar waves in a carefully controlled manner, so that virtually no energy is reflected toward the transmitter. Bill Sweetman

fore require a bigger, more complex inlet in order to meet Stealth objectives, and its performance advantage would be wiped out or reversed.

The inlets take the form of S-ducts which project through the upper skin of the wing. Their curious shape, composed of Gothic triangles, is reflected in the shallow secondary scoops built into the wing just ahead of the main inlets, which swallow the turbulent air next to the wing surface before it can disrupt flow in the duct.

The engine exhausts are the primary battlefield in the war against infrared detection. There are many types of infrared sensor in service, and their different capabilities are sometimes confused. The basic fact is that the atmosphere absorbs infrared energy. At a range of a few miles, a small infrared sensor can receive enough energy to produce a TV-type image of the scene; at greater ranges, this capability is much diminished. Most medium-to-long-range systems, such as the infrared search and track systems (IRSTS) fitted to Soviet interceptors and the homing heads of infrared-guided missiles, do not detect the infrared emissions from the aircraft itself, but the radiation from the hot air and water vapor emitted by its engines.

The B-2's exhausts are built into the top of the wing. The primary nozzles are well ahead of the trailing edge, and lead into a pair of soft-lipped trenches which flare outward. The key to degrading the performance of IRSTS is to ensure that the exhaust dissipates as quickly as possible after leaving the aircraft. To this end, it is likely that the engines are fitted with flow mixers to blend the cold bypass air with the hot air that passes through the combustor and the turbine. The considerable amount of cold boundary layer that is swallowed by the secondary inlets is probably injected into the exhaust stream to cool it further. The exhausts are wide and flat, rather than round; the perimeter of the exhaust is longer than the perimeter of a round exhaust stream, and mixing takes place more quickly. Finally, the interaction between the exhaust stream and the airflow over the aircraft, at each angled side of the exhaust "trench," probably creates a vortex which further promotes mixing.

Acoustic, smoke and contrail signatures also mainly affect the design of the propulsion system. In the acoustic area, the main challenge is, perhaps, the possibility that an adversary could install an interlinked chain of highly sensitive microphones. However, an engine installation such as the B-2's, with a sinuous inlet and an exhaust mixer, is likely to be naturally quiet. Reducing visible smoke is largely a matter of efficient design in the combustion section of the engine.

Contrail control is a different problem. As long ago as the fifties, the USAF experimented with systems which injected a chemical, chloro-fluoro-sulfonic acid, into the exhaust system. The effect of the chemical was to break down the water molecules in the exhaust to a size below the wavelength of white light, making them invisible. The chemical was highly corrosive, and a better system may well have been found for the B-2.

The means by which the B-2's visual signatures are controlled are equally obscure. Head-on views of the YB-49 show that the flying wing's profile dimin-

Antennas for the Hughes radar are installed in the leading edge. They are probably physically fixed, at least in azimuth, and are electronically scanned. The radar is de-signed to track small targets while avoiding detection. The edge of the crew boarding hatch is visible behind the antenna. Bill Sweetman

Composite materials are delivered in the form of "pre-preg" (tape or fabric, impregnated with the matrix which will bind the fibers together). Here, pre-preg is being prepared for use in a process called "pultrusion," in which pre-preg is pulled through a heated die to form components such as channel sections. Lockheed

ishes to a slender line at a distance. The B-2's gray finish blends with the dark, high-altitude sky, further reducing detection range.

Materials

The complex three-dimensional curves of the inlets and the other components are one strong clue to what the B-2 is made of. If they were made in metal, they would be a production engineer's nightmare.

Like its German forebear, the Horten HoIX, the B-2 is made from composite materials. The difference is that the Horten machine's composites grew on trees and the B-2's come from a chemical plant.

Composites

Wood is a composite, and so is fiberglass; both consist of fibers with high tensile strength, bonded together by a matrix material which gives the material resistance to buckling under compression. In the sixties, however, scientists produced new artificial fibers, such as graphite (also called carbon) and DuPont's Kevlar, which were both stronger and less elastic than glass, and which could therefore be used for highly loaded airplane structures.

Stronger and lighter than aluminum alloys, resistant to fatigue and unaware of the meaning of the word corrosion, composites are gradually taking over much of the aerospace industry. The B-2 is a very important milestone in this process, being ten times as large as any previous all-composite aircraft.

RCS factor

The B-2's structure also plays an important role in its Stealth characteristics. Two steps in reducing the RCS of an airplane have already been described: the choice of a low-RCS configuration and the development and implementation of complex shaping laws. The third and final step is the use of special materials to further attenuate radar waves. Radar-absorbent material (RAM) applies to a whole class of materials in different forms which are designed specifically to do this. Radar-absorbing structure (RAS) involves building these materials into load-bearing structure.

All RAM and RAS work on the same basic principle. Radar signals are electromagnetic waves, and ·bounce efficiently off any conductive object. However, the electromagnetic characteristics of different objects and materials are not the same. One of the best dem-

This is not a runway, but an outdoors RCS testing range. An aircraft or a model is mounted on a pylon at one end of the strip, and a radar is installed at the other. Outdoor ranges can be used to test large models at real-world wavelengths, but wind, rain and security are a problem. Martin-Marietta

onstrations of this principle is the domestic microwave oven.

The microwave oven is based on a powerful, crude magnetron, a radar-wave generator which was invented during World War II and which made British and American radars decisively superior to their German counterparts. It is no coincidence that one of the major brands of microwave is called a Radarange and is made by a division of Raytheon, which makes radars and radar-guided missiles. The device was invented by radar engineers who had observed its effects.

RAM

While some substances reflect radar waves efficiently, others do not. The difference lies in their molecular structure. Some materials, including many organic substances (such as foodstuffs), include "free electrons" in their molecular chains. Electrical engineers call them "lossy." Radars, like radios and televisions, operate on a given wavelength; in the case of most radars, the wavelength is measured in gigahertz (GHz), or billions of cycles per second. When a radar transmitter illuminates an object with such characteristics, the free electrons are forced to oscillate back and forth at the frequency of the radar wave. But these particles have friction and inertia, however tiny, and the process is not one hundred percent efficient. The radar's energy is transformed into heat, and the chicken is cooked or (depending what modern folk myth is being repeated) the poodle explodes or your underwear catches fire. These substances are "lossy dielectrics" because they are non-conductive.

Other materials, including glass, ceramics and many plastics, are simply "dielectric." They do not conduct electricity and radar waves pass straight through them with minimum reflection or absorption, even at high power levels. This is why such materials are used in microwave utensils.

Indoor RCS ranges use small-scale models and small-scale radar waves, produced by sources in the millimeter-wave band. The chambers and model-support pylons are lined with carbon-loaded styrofoam pyramids. However, scaling effects are always a problem, and small-scale ranges are not used to validate final designs. LTV

Another major group is the "lossy magnetic" materials, typically iron compounds called ferrites. A radar wave induces a magnetic field in the ferrite material, but the field must switch polarity at the radar frequency. As in the case of the lossy dielectric, this process is not one hundred percent efficient and much of the energy is transformed into heat.

The early types of RAM developed in World War II were lossy dielectrics, mostly using carbon as the active ingredient. (The production version of the Horten HoIX was to have been skinned in a sandwich material with powdered

Many of the dark areas on this unpainted B-1 are dielectric panels over antennas, such as the nose radome and the large radome on the leading edge, which cover elements of the electronic warfare system.

Others are RAM. Potential corner reflectors, such as the blade antennas on the fuselage and the ride-control vanes below the windshield, are among the treated areas. Rockwell

This view shows RAM on the trailing edges and wings of the B-1B. The slot into which the wing moves as it sweeps back was redesigned when the B-1B was developed from

the B-1A, to incorporate a new radar-absorbent inflatable seal developed by Woodville Polymers in England. Rockwell

charcoal in its core.) Carbon-loaded styrofoam, shaped into pyramids for optimum effect, is still the material of choice for lining anechoic chambers, used to test electronic equipment, but is hardly suitable for most other applications.

RAM has been available for years in many forms, and many of them are not even classified. Most such material consists of an active ingredient—a dielectric, such as carbon, or magnetic ferrites—which is molded into a non-lossy dielectric matrix, usually a plastic of some kind. Lockheed developed a lossy plastic material for the A-12 and D-21. Goodyear (now Loral Defense Systems) has provided a material that resembles a ferrite-loaded neoprene, which is used in the inlet ducts of the B-1. A ferrite-

based paint known as "iron ball" is used on the SR-71.

Some basic limitations apply in some degree to all kinds of RAM. All of them absorb a portion of the radar energy and reflect the rest. A given type of RAM is also most effective at a certain frequency and less so at others. Similarly, the effectiveness of RAM varies with the angle of the incident radar wave. Generally, too, the thickness and weight of RAM increases with its effectiveness. Ideal RAM has been described as "paint-like, broadband, unaffected by incidence angle and impervious to climate," but this objective is on a par with "a dog that neither barks nor bites, eats broken glass and excretes diamonds."

Honeycomb

RAS is more complicated, more recent in origin and more classified. However, the essential principle seems to be a "defense in depth" against radar waves, to achieve a high degree of absorption over a wide bandwidth. Except in a case of dire need, nobody is going to cover an airplane with a thick, solid skin. The alternative means of providing the necessary depth is to use "honeycomb" structure. It is worth noting that in 1986, as the B-2 manufacturing base was being built, the Hexcel Corporation established a new, secure facility for its Advanced Products Division in Tempe, Arizona. Hexcel is the leading supplier of honeycomb to the aerospace industry. Other features of the B-2 (notably, its extremely thick landing gear doors) point to the use of honeycomb.

Honeycomb is so called because it looks like honeycomb, a piece of structural magic borrowed from nature. Its core is made of a light fiber material,

The main landing gears retract forward and upward, and each is covered by one very large, thick door. The door's thickness and its smooth inner surface strongly suggest honeycomb construction. Bill Sweetman

such as DuPont's Nomex, bonded together in such a way that it forms a flexible slab with hexagonal passages from front to back. Load-bearing skins, which can be relatively light and flexible, are then bonded to the front and back of the slab. The result is a panel across which you can drive a truck without breaking it, and an aircraft skin which needs no stiffeners or stringers.

From the viewpoint of RAS, the advantage of honeycomb is depth without proportionate weight. A honeycomb RAS might consist of an outer skin of Kevlar 149/epoxy composite, which is transparent to radar, and an inner skin of reflective graphite/epoxy. The Nomex core, between them, would be treated with an absorbent agent, increasing in density from front to rear of the honeycomb.

The front-face reflection of such an RAS would be minimal. As the radar wave encounters the thinly spread absorber on the outer edges of the core, a small part of its energy is absorbed and a small part scattered. As the wave proceeds through the core, it encounters more densely loaded core material which both absorbs and reflects more energy. But before the reflected energy can reach free space again, it is once more attenuated by the outermost layer of absorber. It is an electromagnetic Roach Motel—radar waves check in, but they don't check out.

It is quite likely that the B-2 uses honeycomb RAS in parts of its structure. It also seems to use non-structural RAM on its wing leading edges and wingtips, inside its air inlets and around its exhausts. The combination of the flying-wing shape, Northrop's low-RCS shaping laws and RAM/RAS made it possible for Northrop to predict, back in the early stages of the program, that the bomber would demonstrate a massive reduction in reflectivity, approaching three orders of magnitude. If a nominal target had an RCS of 10 square meters, therefore, the B-2 would have an RCS of 0.01 square meters, equivalent to that of a small bird. A radar with a range of 200 miles against the standard aircraft would not detect the B-2 until it was thirty-five miles away.

Design by computer

The snag with the B-2 design was that it was virtually impossible to produce using existing technology, and that it would be prohibitively expensive to build if it could be built at all. This was because Northrop's concept for RCS control was unforgiving. The external shape of every aircraft had to conform exactly to the low-RCS shape defined by the supercomputers, and everything had to fit perfectly. Electromagnetic laws, it seemed, were even less tolerant of deviation than aerodynamics.

The shape of a conventional aircraft is basically defined in terms of stations, which are cross-sectional views of the aircraft taken at different points from nose to tail or from wingtip to wingtip. After the aircraft is designed on paper in this way, the production engineers use these stations to define three-dimensional parts, interpreting the drawings to fill in the shape between stations. This is acceptable for aerodynamic purposes, but apparently not for Stealth.

Northrop's solution was to complete a revolution in design and manufacture which had started in the early seventies. The development of computers, graphic

Inside Northrop's engineering citadel at Pico Rivera, California. This design office does not contain a single drawing board; instead, engineers work at computer terminals. The six controls at the side of each screen control the cursor and zoom and rotate the image on the screen.

displays and other tools had reached a point by the end of the decade where many engineers worked at a computer screen rather than a drawing board. A CAD (computer aided design) system allows the designer to change the drawing on the screen, change its scale, visualize it from different points and rotate it.

On the assembly line, more and more tasks were being undertaken by automated machines guided by computers. Machining, riveting, building up laminates from layers of graphite fiber tape were being or could be carried out under electronic control, with great consistency and the potential for built-in inspection.

With a new, very long, valuable program ahead of it, Northrop had the opportunity to adopt a completely new way of doing business. As the company renovated the massive plant at Pico Rivera, where much of the B-2 was to be built, it did so according to a new concept called computer integrated manufacturing (CIM).

At Pico Rivera, the image of computer-aided design became the reality. The first and most difficult job was to define the external shape of the new bomber on the computer database, not in terms of sections and stations, but in its totality. The database contained the precise three-dimensional coordinates of any point on the skin. The database was housed on banks of tape drives and managed by a Cray supercomputer.

Connected to the database were more than 400 computer work stations at Pico Rivera; the database was shared with major subcontractors Boeing and Vought and their own engineers.

As detail design proceeded, the engineers could work from the outside in; as the design of each part was completed, it was added to the database. The computer system grew to define the shape and location of every component of the B-2, quite literally down to the smallest fastener.

Actually, according to sources close to the program, this detail is not difficult to achieve once the system is in place. Since many small parts (fasteners and couplings, for example) are identical, the database needs to store their complete characteristics only once, storing only the location and orientation of the individual parts.

The same database is used to control machine tools and industrial robots, to design tooling and forms, and to generate data for tooling alignment. An engineer developing an operating program for a machine tool, for example, can do so on a CAD work station, drawing on the actual characteristics of the component itself. The engineer no longer has to re-interpret another engineer's drawing. The same applies to automatic tape-laying and other composite manufacturing processes.

Quite early in the program, the database took over from the first "engineering fixture" produced to support the B-2 design, so that the aircraft became the first of such complexity to be created without a true mock-up. The mock-up, a full-size model of a new airplane, has long been a symbol of human imperfectibility in engineering. It's a cumbersome device, but necessary to prevent gross errors (such as one engineer's hydraulic tube running through another's firebottle), and to catch some of the smaller fit problems. The database not only replaces the mock-up in this respect, but does so better. The engineer can visualize interference problems on the screen as the component takes shape; before the design is released, it is run through a validation process which checks every point against the database. "First-part" fit errors have been reduced by a factor of six compared with previous programs, eliminating a great deal of tedious and costly reworking of not-quite-right components.

The computer system has opened the way to a change which is as much cultural as it is technological. Most program managers now assert that manufacturing and logistics engineers are involved in the design process. They ensure, for example, that components are designed in a way that lends itself to automation, and that components are

readily accessible. Within the B-2 program, however, the manufacturing and logistics groups can review engineering progress in near-real time; because of this, they can be, and have been, given authority over design release. The engineers alone cannot release a component over the objections of manufacturing or logistics. Instead, the different groups cooperate on the design and, through NCAD, can implement a producibility or supportability improvement two to five times faster than using a conventional drafting method. Northrop people are now carrying this cultural change into the California education system, pressing the aeronautical-engineering departments to lay more stress on production technology.

In a very real sense, the database *is* the B-2, and the airplanes on the pro-

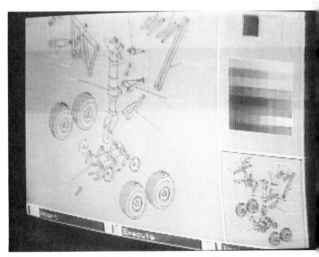

The computer-aided design system allows the engineer to zoom and rotate a view such as this, closing in on the most minute details. More important is the fact that this graphic is drawn from a single vast database which encompasses the entire B-2 design.

Technology to form large, complex components out of composites is readily available. This large wing section was produced by Boeing as part of its early work on the Advanced Tactical Fighter program. Boeing

Driven directly by the central database, an automated tape-laying machine at Boeing assembles a spar for the B-2. The process is highly predictable and can be accurately repeated for any number of components, produced over any period of time.

duction line are a representation of it, along with the electronic instruction codes for the robots, illustrations for logistics manuals and models for wind-tunnel and RCS testing.

Specifications

Ultimately, though, the USAF is not buying a database, but a bomber, and it is on its performance as a bomber that the B-2 must justify its immense cost. It is perhaps not surprising that the B-2's performance figures are classified (apart from the fairly obvious fact that it is not supersonic), as are other details (such as its weight) which would provide clues to its capabilities. However, some rough estimates can be made.

The B-2 is so radical in its design that it is extremely difficult to estimate its physical characteristics and performance with any great degree of confidence. It is completely different in shape from any modern aircraft which performs the same mission. And the only aircraft of comparable shape and size was designed more than forty years ago.

The YB-49, however, possessed precisely the same wingspan as the B-2, which may make some rough comparisons realistic. While the B-49's maximum take-off weight was 213,000 pounds, Jack Northrop estimated that the wing's volume would allow a weight of 300,000 pounds or more (something which might have been achieved through artificial stability, as noted earlier). The B-2, despite its thinner-section outer wings and tapered wingtips, has significantly more internal volume than the older design and its weight limit is accordingly higher. Its flaps should allow it to take off comfortably at high weights, even though the bomber's wing loading will be low compared to that of current conventional subsonic aircraft.

The General Electric F118-GE-100 engines fitted to the B-2 develop 19,000 pounds thrust each, some fifteen percent more than the dry rating of the F110 from which they are derived. Most large modern aircraft have thrust/weight ratios in the region of 0.25:1 to 0.28:1, which would place the B-2's gross weight between 270,000 pounds and 300,000 pounds. However, as Northrop noted in 1947, the all-wing aircraft requires less power in cruise than does a conventional design of the same mass, because of its lower drag. Lockheed studies of span-loaded freighters in the seventies suggested that they could achieve performance similar to conventional aircraft with ten percent less power.

A multipurpose tool at LTV's Advanced Composites Center works on a large airframe section for the B-2, drilling, deburring and installing fasteners in one operation. Special nonmetallic fasteners have been developed for the B-2 and other Stealth aircraft.

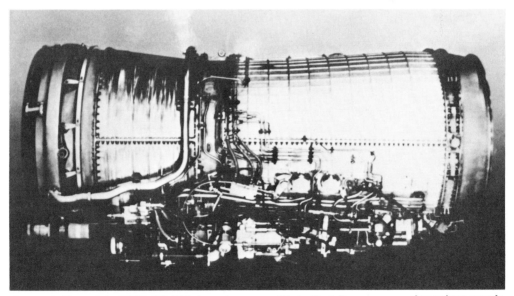

General Electric's F118-GE-100 is externally very similar to the F110 fighter engine, from which it was derived. However, it is *likely that it uses a complex mixer nozzle, not fitted to the engine in this photograph.*

The B-2's size and thrust, therefore, suggest a gross weight in the region of 325,000 to 350,000 pounds, or possibly a little more. Again, mid-seventies studies of span-loaded aircraft suggested that empty weight could be reduced from the forty to fifty percent of normal take-off weight which is typical of conventional subsonic aircraft to less than thirty-five percent. This would set the B-2's empty weight at around 105,000 to 120,000 pounds, an interesting comparison with the 89,000 pound figure for the YB-49.

Taking account of major technological advances on the one hand, and the new bomber's greater weight, bulk and speed on the other, such a comparison may not be unreasonable. We know, also, that the B-2's payload of sixteen SRAM II missiles or B83 nuclear bombs weighs about 40,000 pounds.

If these figures are anywhere near being accurate, the B-2 emerges with an internal fuel capacity of 180,000 to 200,000 pounds with maximum weapons, and a fuel fraction (the portion of

Rotary weapons launchers were first developed for the SRAM missile in the sixties. All the complex umbilical connections required for the arming, safing and control of missiles and nuclear bombs can be routed through the launcher spindle, rather than being split along two sides of a conventional
bomb bay; and all connections can be designed to separate vertically. If a weapon fails an inflight test, it can be retained without blocking the release of other weapons. This is a Common Strategic Rotary Launcher (CSRL) for a B-52H.

the gross weight available for fuel, and an important influence on range) around fifty-five percent. This is roughly equal to the fuel fraction of the much larger B-52H with an equal bombload.

A B-52H in that configuration has a high-altitude radius of action around 4,260 miles; the B-2, with a substantially lower drag coefficient and more modern engines, should be at least twenty to twenty-five percent better, with an unre-fueled radius of action around 5,200 miles. The USAF's claim that the B-2 will be able to operate with less tanker sup-

port than current bombers appears to be justified.

The critical difference between the B-2 and the B-52H, however, is that the older aircraft's range at high altitude is almost academic, because it must drop to lower levels in order to survive in defended airspace. Stealth technology, which reduces radar detection range to the same degree as low-altitude flight, will allow this full high-altitude range to be used operationally.

The B-2 will probably cruise around Mach 0.8 to 0.85, or eighty to eighty-five

Internal view of the XB-35 shows how the principles of all-wing design have changed remarkably little over the years. Major components are still spread along the wingspan, and the structure is bulky, but efficient and light. In order to reduce weight and approach as closely as possible to the ideal all-wing shape, the Northrop designers spread the weapon load out in six small bays, none of which could accommodate a weapon larger than a 4,000 pound bomb. Early atomic bombs were considerably larger and the XB-35 could not carry them. Northrop

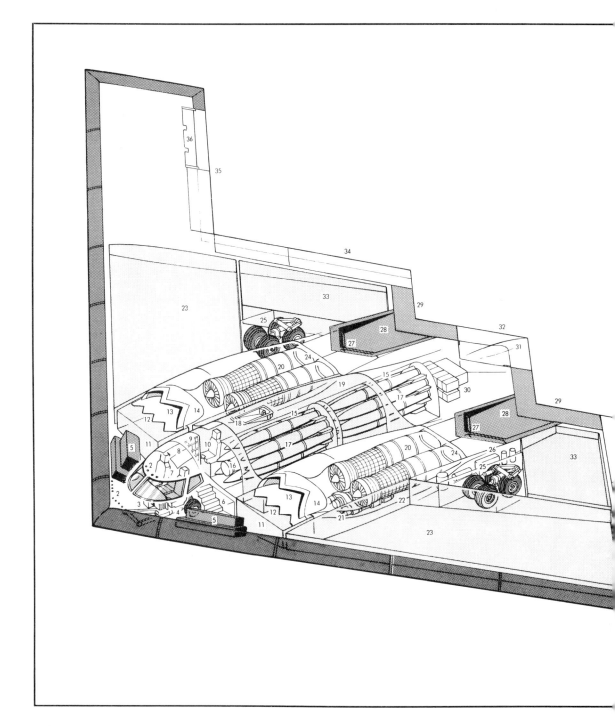

KEY
1. *Leading-edge radar-absorbent material*
2. *Air-data sensors*
3. *Multi-CRT instrument panel*
4. *Nose landing gear stowage*
5. *Hughes Covert Strike Radar, port and starboard*
6. *Crew entry via ventral hatch*
7. *Two-crew cockpit*
8. *Escape hatches*
9. *Avionics racks, port and starboard*
10. *Provision for third crew seat*
11. *Forward fuel tanks*
12. *Boundary-layer splitter*
13. *Engine air intakes*
14. *Intake internal plenum*
15. *Twin tandem weapons bays*
16. *Advanced Applications Rotary Launcher (AARL)(2)*
17. *AGM-131 SRAM II air-to-surface missiles, total 16 (B83 bombs alternative*
18. *Inflight refuelling receptacle*
19. *Center-fuselage fuel tank*
20. *General Electric F118-GE-100 non-afterburning turbofan engines*
21. *Airframe-mounted accessory equipment gearbox*
22. *Bypass air duct*
23. *Main wing fuel tanks*
24. *Exhaust duct mixer*
25. *Main landing gear stowage*
26. *Hydraulic and electrical equipment bays, port and starboard*
27. *Conformal exhaust nozzles*
28. *Carbon-carbon upper surface exhaust duct*
29. *Trailing-edge exhaust deflectors*
30. *Aft avionics equipment racks*
31. *Tail radome*
32. *Adjustable boat tail for gust alleviation*
33. *Trailing edge fuel tanks*
34. *Inboard flaps/elevons*
35. *Outboard flaps/elevons*
36. *Spoiler panels*
37. *Honeycomb composite skin panelling*

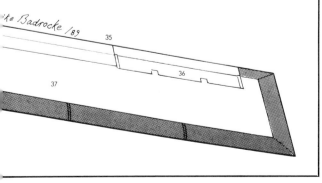

percent of the speed of sound. This is equivalent to 530 to 560 mph. Cruising significantly faster than this increases drag and fuel consumption, and reduces range. The bomber should have a respectable high-altitude performance, in contrast to the B-1. The B-2's wing is much bigger, both in span and in area, and it has slightly more cruise thrust than the B-1, but it weighs much less. It should be able to cruise at 55,000 feet without difficulty. Again, while high-altitude flight has been out of fashion since the early sixties, Stealth makes it viable again. The advantage of a higher cruising altitude is that it enables the bomber's sensors to scan a wider area.

Stealth, vectored thrust, composite materials and robotic manufacture make the B-2 an astonishing blend of technologies. No nation, however, can afford $70 billion to field an airplane unless it has a mission. The purpose of the B-2 is to drop nuclear bombs. Thirty years after the first intercontinental missiles entered service, why does the USAF still believe that it needs bombers?

Internal layout of the B-2 shows how the long-chord, deep-section center structure accommodates the bomber's weapon load, its engines, its crew and most other systems, while still providing space for an enormous amount of fuel, which gives the B-2 its remarkable range and endurance. The S-shaped inlet ducts mask the all-metal engines from radar. This drawing is based on analysis of the best available photographs. Mike Badrocke

Chapter 5

Weapons of Armageddon

Peace is our profession.

*Motto of Strategic Air Command, the most powerful force of destruction
in the world's history*

Nobody likes to discuss the purpose of nuclear weapons in polite company. There is a chasm between the theologians of nuclear warfare, who deal in targets, yields and countermeasures, and the rational layperson, who views nuclear warfare as the ultimate nightmare. The fact that both sides are right does not help to narrow the gulf between them.

Unless we want to argue the case for the abolition of all nuclear weapons, however, we have to embark on a discussion of why some systems are more effective than others. And we enter into the vocabulary and world of the nuclear theologians—whether or not we share their fundamental beliefs.

At enormous cost, the United States maintains three different classes of weapon which threaten, or, as the Air Force says, "hold at risk" targets within the Soviet heartland. SAC has its bombers and its intercontinental ballistic missile (ICBM) systems: the veteran

Minuteman and the new Peacekeeper, formerly known as MX. The ICBMs are housed in underground concrete bunkers called silos, protected against nuclear blast and radiation. The US Navy has its submarine-launched ballistic missile (SLBM) systems. The original Polaris was followed by Poseidon; this was in turn replaced by Trident, carried on new and much larger *Ohio*-class submarines.

The arguments for maintaining these different kinds of weapons have changed over the years with shifting priorities and changing targets. In the early days of nuclear weapons, the bombs and the bombers which would drop them were regarded in much the same light as the bombers of World War II. They would be sent out to destroy both industrial and military targets, attacking both the enemy's means and the will to fight.

In the early days of the ICBM, bomber advocates argued that the missiles of the day could put nowhere near as many megatons on target as a bomber. They were also much less accurate. The ICBM relied solely on an inertial guid-ance system, which would drift off course simply because no mechanical system is perfect. Its accuracy also depended on the accuracy with which the relative positions of the launch point and the target could be determined, which in itself was not easy. Available charts of

A USAF/Boeing Minuteman III ICBM is fired from Vandenberg AFB. Vulnerable to destruction on the ground, missiles are almost immune after launch. Boeing

The lethality of missiles, particularly against ICBM silos, dramatically increased when multiple, independently targeted re-entry vehicles (MIRVs) replaced single war-heads in the early seventies. Three 335 kiloton Mark 12A MIRVs are seen on a Minuteman III "bus," which releases the warheads at separate, predetermined points on its trajectory through space. The MX and D5 missiles carry ten MIRVs each. Los Alamos National Laboratory via Chuck Hansen

the Soviet Union dated back to the Tsars, and were not based on the same geodetic coordinates as other charts of the day. The CEP (circular error probable) of the missile (the circle within which half the missiles aimed at any point could be expected to land) was around 800 to 1,000 yards in diameter. To destroy any kind of hardened target, therefore, the missile needed a massive warhead, so early missiles were large and expensive.

The SLBM had the same problems of accuracy, compounded by the fact that it was launched from a moving platform. The early Polaris also had a limited range and could carry only a small warhead. Unlike the larger land-based missiles, therefore, Polaris could not compensate for reduced accuracy with a massive warhead, and was consequently of little use against most military objectives.

Simple economics further protected the bomber in the early sixties. Missiles, silos and submarines were expensive, and it would be years, at any practical rate of construction and installation, before enough missiles could be built to cover the targets held at risk by SAC's hundreds of bombers.

But missile technology galloped ahead in the sixties while bomber development stagnated. Missile inertial guidance systems improved immensely, having the CEP. It was realized that a number of small bombs would do more damage than one huge one (like the nine-megaton W53 carried by the Titan). The Minuteman III and sea-launched Poseidon, entering service in the early seventies, were the first missiles to carry multiple independently targeted re-entry vehicles (MIRVs). The small, conical MIRVs—with a typical yield of around 150 to 200 kilotons (KT)—were attached to a maneuverable "bus" which released each MIRV separately as it followed a pre-programmed track through space. The argument that it was impossible to afford enough missiles to cover every target was rapidly crumbling.

MAD

Technical developments in nuclear weapons were closely related to the changes in nuclear strategy which took place in the fifties and sixties. Despite successive scares over a "bomber gap" in the mid-fifties, and a "missile gap" a few years later, it was not until the mid-sixties that the Soviet Union began to field a nuclear striking force comparable to that of the United States. Robert McNamara was the first US Secretary of Defense to face this situation. Influenced by strategists at the RAND Corporation, a USAF-funded think tank, McNamara adopted a principle first identified as "assured destruction." It was later known as "mutual assured destruction" or MAD.

MAD was intended to make it entirely clear to both sides that no nuclear attack, no matter how efficiently planned or executed, would be anything but suicidal. Whatever happened, the attacker could never destroy all the victim's nuclear weapon systems, and what remained would be enough to destroy the aggressor nation.

MAD also introduced the phrases "first strike" and "second strike" into the public debate. First strike was the surprise attack, and it was naturally considered important to deny the potential enemy the ability to launch such an attack with any hope of success. Second strike was the retaliatory attack. In this case, the concern was to ensure that the ability to launch a second strike would be retained in the worst possible circumstances.

What made MAD a very stable strategy was the relatively poor accuracy of ICBMs, and the hardness of their silos. Given contemporary technology, it would take several ICBMs to guarantee destruction of one on the ground. For a successful first strike, an attacker would need several times more missiles than the target country, and it would be physically and economically impossible to establish such an advantage. And even so, there were always submarines to deliver the retaliatory blow.

From the viewpoint of MAD, the best weapon system was as invulnerable as possible before launch and not particularly accurate. If it was inaccurate, it could not be used in a first strike against the other side's weapon systems. The SLBM filled the bill almost perfectly. It was more expensive than the ICBM. Ballistic missile submarines are vulnerable in port and are only effective when

An Ohio-*class submarine is a seagoing missile base, bigger than most of the US Navy's surface ships. When the D5 missile is deployed in the nineties, each* Ohio *class submarine will be armed with up to 240 accurate, 375 kiloton nuclear warheads.* General Dynamics

they are at sea. After each patrol, they must be taken down for long refits, so a nation must build two submarines for every one on station. Submarines are vulnerable to destruction during a period of conventional war, unlike home-land-based bombers and ICBMs. While encouraging the development of SLBMs, McNamara continued the development of ICBMs.

Triad

McNamara's successor under the Nixon Administration, Melvin Laird, had written a book before taking office, out-lining his belief that the Soviet Union was gearing up for a surprise nuclear attack against the United States. In office, he adopted the MAD doctrine but added to it a new concept, called the Triad.

Triad saw deterrence standing on three legs: ICBMs, SLBMs and the bomb-er force, any one of them capable of delivering a second strike that would threaten military targets and command centers. The differences between the systems were highlighted, and presented as advantages of the entire Triad rather than in terms of a contest between one system and another. ICBMs were the least costly and most secure against conventional assault; SLBMs, although they were least effective against military targets, were least vulnerable to nuclear attack; and bombers could be launched at a time of tension and then recalled.

Triad was a virtually ironclad guar-antee against an effective first strike, one that worked even if ICBM and MIRV developments reached the point where an attacker could count on one ICBM killing one silo. This concept was based

on the assumption that the United States, the victim of a first strike, would not launch ICBMs merely on warning of an attack, but only after missiles had started to arrive. Bombers, on the other hand, could be launched on warning and recalled in the case of a false alarm.

If the Soviet Union launched ICBMs in a surprise attack, they would be detected as soon as they left their silos and a percentage of the bomber force (a large one if the force was on alert) would be airborne before they arrived. The Soviet planners could, alternatively, attack SAC bomber bases with low-trajectory SLBMs launched as closely as possible to the Atlantic coast, which would arrive much more quickly and allow fewer bombers to leave the ground. However, they could not do both. The SLBMs would hit long before the ICBMs arrived, and the United States could launch its full ICBM force.

In either case, accurate strikes could be directed against military targets and American SLBMs would be kept in reserve. It was, simply, impossible to achieve an optimum first strike on both the bomber and ICBM legs of the Triad. This was a major argument in favor of the B-1, and was frequently advanced during the debate over the aircraft in the seventies.

The strength of the Triad concept has diminished in the eighties, mainly because the US Navy's new D5 or Trident II missile is accurate enough to strike hardened targets. Its long range means that the submarines can patrol in a larger proportion of the world's oceans and are much safer from attack. With 240 warheads on each submarine (com-pared with sixteen on the original Polaris boats) the Trident submarines can form both a secure second-strike force and a reserve.

At that point, the critics of the penetrating bomber argue, "all that the bomber will do is re-arrange the rubble." If the unique attributes of the manned bomber, such as its ability to be recalled, are still required, or if it is considered essential to force the Soviet Union to maintain its air defenses, an "air-breathing" force may be justified, but it is much cheaper to develop such a force around long-range air-launched cruise missiles.

Arms control

But this argument is still grounded in the doctrine of massive retaliation; the all-out exchange in which every nuclear weapon is unleashed at the adversary in the shortest practical time. The modern justification for the bomber rests on very different thinking. Some of it is embodied in war plans which are classified. Most of the time, it is not discussed because most people have sealed the thought of nuclear war in a bunker in a corner of their minds. To put it as baldly as possible, the manned penetrating bomber is designated not for an "exchange," but to fight a war using nuclear weapons.

There has always been one glaring problem with the doctrine of massive retaliation or MAD: there was no sign, from Soviet actions or writings, that it was accepted in the Soviet Union. Soviet ICBMs of the late sixties were clearly being developed for counter-force strikes, with greater accuracy than they needed to strike population centers. The Soviet Union also devoted at least equal energy to its land-based missiles—accu-

rate, but vulnerable to a US first strike— as it did to its less vulnerable but less lethal SLBMs which, as noted earlier, were considered to be the most stable of second-strike weapons. Meanwhile, Soviet civil-defense efforts, such as the construction of shelters beside government and industrial buildings, continued on a much larger scale than any similar preparations in the West.

The United States continued to negotiate with the Soviet Union on arms-control agreements in the late sixties and early seventies, based on the premise that there was no role for nuclear weapons except to threaten annihilation. Because of this, the theory continued, it was in the interests of both the United States and Soviet Union to keep deterrence as stable as possible. One of the first concrete results of this theory was the 1972 Anti-Ballistic Missile (ABM) treaty, which severely limited the deployment and development of systems to shoot down incoming ICBMs and SLBMs. (Systems to destroy bombers were not included.) Subsequently, the US and the Soviet Union agreed to limit the numbers of ballistic missiles that they possessed, under the Strategic Arms Limitation Treaty (SALT).

By the later seventies, with the dovish administration of President Jimmy Carter in power, some theorists and politicians were voicing fears that arms control was a trap set by the Soviet Union. Intelligence reports were leaked to the press, describing massive Soviet civil-defense programs and work on futuristic "beam weapons" capable of destroying ballistic missiles in flight, as well as the Soviet Union's continued development of many different types of

ICBM and SLBM, in pursuit of greater payload and accuracy within SALT limits.

It seemed to some observers that the Soviet Union, having managed to enshrine a form of nuclear parity through arms control, was aiming at superiority; an imbalance of offensive forces and passive defenses which a desperate leadership, facing an uncontrollable crisis, might use to fight a nuclear war. There was no doubt that both sides would suffer immense losses, but the side with superior attack forces, more shelters and some defensive systems might suffer much less and would come through with its social and political structure intact. Whether MAD would always remain mutual, as had once been assumed, was in doubt.

What is nuclear war?

An imbalance of power at the level of total annihilation raised a lower-level question. Nuclear-war theorists of the late fifties had coined the term "escalation" to describe the process by which a first use of a small battlefield nuclear weapon could lead to a global nuclear war as the two sides traded progressively heavier blows. Escalation theory also explained how this could be avoided. If neither side could rely on a favorable outcome at any level on the escalation ladder, the theory went, both would have more to lose than to gain by escalating to that level. This complex doctrine and its implementation were overshadowed in the sixties by the emphasis on MAD, but similar ideas returned to the fore in the late seventies.

If the Soviet Union's strategists refused to accept that massive retaliation was the only possible type of nuclear war, it was hard for the United States, on its own, to maintain the credibility of a posture that was based on that model. What if there was more than one kind of nuclear war? Instead of executing a massive strike using hundreds of missiles, an adversary might fire only a few at a time, at selected targets, perhaps in support of conventional war aims. Command and control facilities might be hit first; alternatively, seaports shipping weapons to a conventional war zone might be targeted, or high-altitude nuclear bursts could be used to disrupt communications and electronic equipment.

How could a national leader respond to such an attack? Would any leader initiate an assault with every ICBM and bomber available in response to an attack by a handful of low-yield warheads on military targets in a sparsely populated area? That was the response demanded by massive retaliation, but it was hard to believe that a President would do it, or to believe that the Soviet Union would necessarily fear such a response. The leader's options would depend entirely on the means available, and a major concern was that the means available, rigidly tailored to an almost-automatic retaliatory strike, did not provide many choices.

In 1967, a RAND strategist summed up the attributes of a nuclear force capable of offering a commander-in-chief such a range of options. While he was writing about European forces, the observations are equally applicable to the long-range arena. They foreshadow, to a remarkable extent, the US nuclear forces that are under development today.

"It requires at the outset a very large force, so that numerous vehicles and weapons can be allocated to strikes at the extended forces of the foe," he wrote. "It requires a hyper-protected force for intra-war deterrence, with long endurance and excellent communications and control. It requires, in the counterforce stage, the ability to assess damage—and to re-assign vehicles—thereby compounding the requirements for the command, control and communications system. It requires knowledge of the deployment of the opponent's forces."

The strategist who wrote these comments was James Schlesinger, who later became Nixon's second Secretary of Defense. The first bomber conceived in the missile era, the B-1, was initially developed under his leadership.

The bomber, with its large warload and ability to attack multiple targets on a single mission, is a valuable asset if "a very large force," in terms of warheads, is a goal. (This attribute of the bomber has been further highlighted by treaty limitations, which treat one bomber, with sixteen- to twenty-four-megaton warheads, as the equivalent of one missile with ten smaller MIRVs.) The replacement of the B-52 with the more powerful and accurate B-1 would clearly be a step on the way to increasing the power of the bomber component. "Intra-war deterrence," or the ability to deter the enemy from doing worse even after nuclear exchanges have started, is another vital concept; it does require excellent communications and control, which are a particularly important at-

tribute of the bomber. As for the ability to assess damage and re-assign vehicles, this had been an element of the USAF's case for the Valkyrie bomber only six years before the Schlesinger report was written.

Thinking about nuclear war in this way has passed well beyond the theoretical stage. Nuclear weapons in both the United States and the Soviet Union are no longer replaced because their replacements are significantly longer-ranging or harder-hitting, as has been the case in the past. They are being replaced by systems which can endure a longer war. The same goes, in an even greater degree, for the command, control, communications and intelligence devices which would support them.

The immediate and rational concern raised by any talk of "theater," "limited" or "controlled" nuclear war is that the reduction in intensity is combined with an increase in probability; as we consider nuclear war as something other than a totally devastating, uncontrolled exchange, we make it more likely to happen. The answer, in the eyes of the professionals, is to maintain forces which deny the adversary any confidence in a favorable outcome, at any level of nuclear war. This means thinking about all the forms which a nuclear exchange could take, and ultimately equipping and training forces to fight a nuclear war which may last days or weeks rather than the minutes of popular belief.

All war is chaos. Nuclear war would spread over much of the world the sort of confusion and wreckage that followed the bloodiest land campaigns of history. A document prepared by Lockheed outlines the company's approach to the Air Force's call for a worldwide flying command post for strategic forces. It describes a modified C-5, hardened against nuclear flash and electromagnetic pulse; remaining airborne for tens of hours; landing at "austere facilities," such as small airports or pre-surveyed desert sites; carrying rest bunks, relief crews, supplies of food and water, and its own HMMVW four-wheel-drive, while its racks of computers monitored the end of the world we know.

Herman Kahn coined the term "spasm warfare" to describe the nuclear conflict that most of us fear. The phrase catches the essence of an uncontrolled expenditure of force. It implies missile after missile erupting from silos or from the sea, followed by the last wait for the first warheads to fall.

But a nuclear war of multiple exchanges is more akin to classic military strategy, where the most basic question facing the commander is whether and when to expend or conserve forces. The arrival of Blucher's fresh regiments sealed Bonaparte's fate at Waterloo. Computer simulations of nuclear war show that the side which retains the larger reserve of operational weapons holds the initiative. This doctrine stresses the importance of a reserve force which can survive repeated attacks and remain operational. This force has to consist of weapons which can both survive and be controlled over a long period, together with a survivable system to control them.

Protecting our targets from attack

The idea of "survivability" in a nuclear war is foreign to most of us, cul-turally inclined to consider nuclear war as total destruction. But there are many things that can be done to protect targets, even in the face of the apocalyptic power of thermonuclear detonations. Images of Hiroshima and Nagasaki tend to obscure the fact that these were cities of delicately built wooden structures, not military targets.

A nuclear weapon releases the atomic energy of its contents in a fireball. The heat of the fireball consumes all known materials and its radiated energy will ignite or melt many materials at close range. The heat pulse diminishes with the square of the distance from the explosion, but can still ignite flammable materials at a considerable distance. The result is that a nuclear explosion would probably cause dozens or hundreds of serious fires, most of which would burn unchecked. However, it is not too difficult to protect a military objective from the effects of flash-caused fires, by establishing firebreaks around it or locating it away from flammable materials, and by making its surface nonflammable.

The nuclear fireball superheats the air around it, which expands violently into plasma and creates the second damage mechanism, the blast wave. This will destroy buildings close to the explosion and damage them at greater range. The blast overpressure declines in proportion to the square of the distance from the explosion.

Bury them

Early thoughts of protecting likely targets from nuclear blast led to the construction of shelters and bunkers. First, strategic command posts were buried. The North American Air Defense

(NORAD) post at Colorado Springs, Colorado, was tunneled into the side of a hard-rock mountain, with massive doors and a complex system of entrance tunnels. The Soviet Union has built deeply buried centers of government and administration under most of its major cities, in a program which started in the fifties.

With the introduction of the ICBM, it seemed logical to put the new weapons in a bunker, too: a protected vertical launch tube or silo. Designed to withstand flash and blast, the shelter or silo could be wrecked by an accurate missile hit. By the seventies, the hardening of the silo was reaching its physical limit, but missile accuracy continued to improve, so that the number of warheads required to ensure the destruction of a silo was shrinking.

Move them

However, there is one way to negate missile accuracy: prevent the adversary from knowing exactly where the target will be at the time of the explosion. An ICBM or SLBM is a very refined dumb weapon, a giant artillery shell. It can maneuver only in space, and it has no sensors to locate its target. Like artillery, it does not aim at a target, but a particular set of coordinates determined by

According to the philosophy of deterrence, all command and control centers must be "held at risk," even deeply buried targets such as this one. This vast three-story complex (based on US intelligence assessments of Soviet facilities) is hundreds of yards underground. US Department of Defense

An MX missile will deliver half its ten warheads within a 300 foot circle centered on their targets. Fifty of these weapons are to be mounted on railroad trains, becoming the first US relocatable missile systems. US Department of Defense

A prototype Hard Mobile Launcher (HML), developed by Boeing and Loral to fire the planned Small ICBM (SICBM), demonstrates its cross-country performance. Crew and control electronics are housed in the tractor and the missile is stowed horizontally in the trailer Boeing

pre-strike reconnaissance. If the target moves between the last effective reconnaissance and the warhead's detonation the missile will not hit it.

Neither does the target have to move very fast or very far. Flash and blast diminish with the square of the distance, and a few miles make a tremendous difference. The target will still have to be protected, but the blast level is so much lower that it is possible to install sufficient protection on a practical vehicle.

One example of such a "relocatable" target is the transporter for the planned Midgetman SICBM (single-warhead intercontinental ballistic missile). Resembling a low-slung semi-trailer truck with cross-country capability, the SICBM transporter has a curved roof, a variable-height suspension and a system of "skirts" on its periphery. When a warhead burst is imminent, the transporter squats down on its suspension and the skirts extend to the ground. It is designed so that a blast wave creates a pumping effect, sucking air from beneath the vehicle so that it clings to the ground like a limpet to a ship. The biggest danger—that the blast wave will tip the vehicle over—is thereby averted without making the vehicle too large to move on the roads.

Such targets are called "relocatable" rather than "mobile" because they do not have to move all the time, simply often enough to throw off the adversary's aim. As a conflict continues, they become harder to attack, because it can be taken for granted that the gathering and handling of reconnaissance information will become many times more difficult.

The most important development in relocatable targets is a result of modern electronics. While it would have been possible to make a relocatable ICBM in the sixties, it would not have been possible to make it accurate or reliable; the vacuum-tube electronics of the day would not have survived the impact of explosion or endured long cross-country trips, while the movements of the vehicle would have introduced unacceptable perturbations into the inertial navigation system.

The submarine is a relocatable system by nature, but it has a number of drawbacks which have dissuaded the Soviet and US strategic forces from placing total reliance on it, despite the increasing accuracy of its weapons. The most important of these is communications.

The submarine does not operate in sovereign waters, and can be sought out and attacked during a period of conventional war, so it must conceal its location in order to survive. It operates in

complete radio silence, and no antenna can be allowed to break the surface. Submarines can receive orders from the national command authority (but cannot reply) by very-low-frequency (VLF) or extremely low frequency (ELF) radio

The Soviet SS-24 is a ten-warhead weapon in the MX class. In its Mod 0 version, it is carried on a railroad train which is disguised to resemble a normal freight train. US Department of Defense

The HML trailer has sloped skirts to resist being tipped over by the blast and has hinged flaps on the side of the skirts. If an attack is imminent, the tractor lowers the trailer level with the ground and stands off.

As the blast wave passes over the trailer, low air pressure opens the flaps on the lee side, pressure drops inside the skirts, and the vehicle is sucked down more firmly to the ground. Boeing

signals, which can penetrate water and be received on a long submerged antenna. Unfortunately, the transmitters for these signals are either very large, above-ground antenna arrays (in the case of ELF) or large aircraft, such as the US Navy's TACAMO, which are themselves vulnerable to conventional attack. Moreover, VLF or ELF communication is very slow.

Because of these communication problems, it is hard to use SLBMs as a true strategic reserve. Even under the most favorable conditions, there is likely to be uncertainty as to which submarines are operational, and which have successfully fired their missiles. Given the probable state of confusion and chaos, it is also difficult to issue new targeting instructions to SLBMs in wartime with great confidence.

The mobile land-based ICBM is free from many of these disadvantages. Im-

The road-mobile SS-25, bigger than the SICBM, is mounted on an extremely large truck. In this impression, it operates in consort with a BTR command vehicle. It does not appear to be as well protected as the SICBM launcher, relying on mobility for survival. US Department of Defense

mune to attack from most of the enemy's conventional forces, the land-based relocatable missile can remain in much closer contact with the C3 network and possesses all the targeting flexibility of the fixed ICBM. The development and deployment of such systems is proceeding in both the United States and the Soviet Union.

The USAF started development of the SICBM in 1983, on the recommendation of President Reagan's Scowcroft Commission, which had been formed to resolve years of debate over different ways of protecting ICBM basing modes. SICBM is a small missile, carrying one warhead of the same type as that carried by the ten-warhead MGM-118A Peacekeeper, and (as noted above) is intended to roam large tracts of land on a highly mobile and protected launcher. It is designed to be as accurate as Peacekeeper, which is to say very accurate indeed.

While the technical problems of the SICBM are soluble, its economic challenges are tougher, because each launcher carries only one warhead. A force of 500 missiles would be far more expensive to acquire and to operate than an equivalent force of fifty Peacekeepers, twenty-five B-52Hs or even thirty B-2s. Faced with years of zero-growth defense budgets, the USAF decided in late 1987 that it had to abandon SICBM, over Congressional objections.

Instead, the USAF proposes to deploy fifty Peacekeeper missiles on railroad cars, which will be disguised to resemble the ninety-foot automobile carriers used by the motor industry. The Peacekeeper RG (rail garrison) missiles will not wander constantly over the

120,000 miles of track which can handle such large, heavy stock, but will be based alongside the land-based missiles at F. E. Warren AFB, Wyoming. In a crisis, they would be dispersed rapidly over the rail system. The system requires a minimum of new components, partly because Peacekeeper was originally designed with such basing modes in mind.

Attacking protected targets

The Soviet Union has been working on relocatable ICBMs for longer than the United States; the most likely reason is that it has more to gain, covering well over twice as much land as the United States and possessing one-sixth of the world's total land area. Relocatable missiles can exploit this asset to the fullest extent.

The first relocatable ICBM to be developed and tested was the Soviet Union's SS-X-15 Scrooge, carried in a tubular container on top of a large tracked vehicle; this weapon was not put into production. It was followed by the SS-X-16 of the seventies. But this weapon also was not put into service as a relocatable ICBM, but was modified with a three-warhead "bus" replacing its third stage to produce the SS-20 intermediate-range ballistic missile. True intercontinental mobile missiles entered service in the mid-eighties: the Minuteman-sized, single-warhead SS-25, which is carried on a large multi-wheeled vehicle, and the larger ten-warhead SS-24 which, in its initial Mod 1 version, is carried on a railroad car. US intelligence services estimate that 300 of each will be deployed by the mid-nineties.

Because they can survive first-strike or second-strike attacks, relocatable missiles can be used as a strategic reserve in a protracted multi-stage nuclear war. Indeed, there is little point in going to the expense of building relocatable missiles if they are to be expended in the first wave of attack and retaliation. This in turn raises the question of whether and how the relocatable targets are to be held at risk.

Use bombers

The USAF does not consider "whether" to be an open question. SAC has been given the task of maintaining the threat to the adversary's nuclear forces, its leadership, its conventional forces and its industry, in that order of priority. To concede sanctuary to Soviet mobile missiles would run counter to this basic doctrine, moving the United States back to the days of massive retaliation.

SAC's view is that the bomber, specifically the B-2, is the only way to threaten mobile targets. With present or foreseeable technology, the bomber is the only long-range system which can find a target at an undetermined position within a defined area, identify it, complete an attack on it while its position is still known and confirm its destruction. All four of these steps are critical to holding a relocatable target at risk, and none can be accomplished reliably with any other combination of systems.

The bomber can find targets because it can carry an array of sensors, backed up by information systems and intelligently managed by its human crew. It can receive information in flight via systems such as the USAF/Lockheed Milstar communications satellite. Described as "a warfighter's comsat," Milstar is specifically designed to carry a low volume of essential traffic, even during a prolonged nuclear war. Cruise missiles are restricted to simpler sensor systems and artificial processing and interpretation, and ballistic missiles cannot, yet, carry any effective sensors or act on their information.

The bomber crew can identify their targets because they can combine information from various sensors (radar, passive electromagnetic, infrared) and can classify the target with an increasing degree of certainty as they approach

it. Because the bomber initiates its attack close to the target, no evasion is possible. The relocatable system's speed is enough to remove it from the immediate impact point of a ballistic missile, but inadequate to escape an SRAM II lobbed from a few tens of miles away.

The B-2 is a particularly important weapon against relocatable targets, in SAC's view, because of its ability to penetrate and survive without using terrain cover. This has two results. First, it allows the bomber's sensors to scan a

Taken not with a camera but with a synthetic-aperture radar (SAR), this view of Philadelphia shows the kind of detail that can be obtained under any weather conditions. Moreover, it was acquired by a Loral

UPD-8 radar, which the Pentagon has cleared for export. Imagery from more modern systems, which is highly classified, will be far more detailed than this. Loral

much larger area than they could do if they were mounted on a low-flying B-1, and this area includes fewer "shadow" zones concealed by terrain. Flying at 50,000 feet, for example, a B-2 should be able to see a target the size of an SS-25 launcher at a distance of 100 miles or more. Second, the ability to survive at medium altitude enables the B-2's already considerable range to be translated into endurance, increasing the area which the bomber can search on a given mission.

The war against the mobile missile is far from won. Even if a B-2 could search for three hours over Central Asia, covering 300,000 square miles of territory, it would cover barely one-thirtieth part of the Soviet land mass. The missiles will be protected, at rest, by anti-radar camouflage nets. The SS-24 trains are disguised (like the Peacekeeper RG) and, no doubt, decoys will be

The typical primary armament of a B-52 comprises four megaton-range weapons, mounted in a "clip" which mates them to the aircraft systems. These bombs are MK28 types. The bomber's ability to deliver these heavy weapons accurately gives it a unique capability against very hard targets. USAF via Chuck Hansen

In the next century, mobile targets might be tracked and designated for the B-2 force by hypersonic reconnaissance aircraft; a recent USAF study has looked at such vehicles for "trans-attack" surveillance. This Lock- *heed impression shows a Mach 5, methane-fueled aircraft powered by four turbo-ramjet engines. It is not completely unrealistic, although a real aircraft would probably have a V-tail. Lockheed*

deployed that resemble SS-25 fire units. Likely approaches to the problem include the maximum use of reconnaissance satellites (such as the radar-carrying Indigo Lacrosse, launched by the space shuttle *Atlantis* in late 1988), both to detect missiles in wartime and to monitor their behavior in peacetime; the development of improved onboard sensors; and the use of high-speed computers to analyze sensor data, recognizing targets and discriminating against decoys.

Relocatable missiles, however, are not the only category of targets to be held at risk by the B-2 fleet. Military and command objectives will also be on the target list. The Soviet Union has exploited the fact that, while a missile silo must be close to the surface of the ground in order to fire, a command bunker may be buried hundreds of feet below the surface. If the ground is hard, the target may be safe from all but the largest surface- or air-bursting warheads. However, the logic of treaty limits on the number of delivery vehicles has caused large unitary ICBM warheads such as the Titan's W53 to be replaced by smaller 200 to 500KT MIRVs which are of limited use against deeply buried targets.

Use satellites

In the first half of the eighties, the US intelligence community, drawing on considerable computerized analysis of the vast amount of satellite imagery of the Soviet Union which had been collected in the previous two decades, concluded that the Soviet program to bury

One of the Space Shuttle's most important missions is to launch classified reconnaissance vehicles such as the Lockheed KH-12 optical satellite and the Martin-Marietta Lacrosse radar surveillance satellite. They are needed to help the B-2 find relocatable targets, but their vulnerability in wartime is a controversial point. NASA

and protect leadership and control facilities had been much more extensive than had been generally recognized. At the same time, research showed that most nuclear weapons, which burst above or on the surface, were less effective against buried targets than earlier studies had suggested. As an emergency measure, SAC pulled many of its old MK53 bombs out of retirement. The last of SAC's multi-megaton weapons, the MK53, had been designed for "laydown" delivery. Dropped from low altitude, the bomb would be decelerated rapidly by a large parachute system so that it would hit the ground without skidding hundreds of yards from the impact point. It would explode after a pre-programmed delay, long enough to allow the carrier aircraft to escape the blast zone.

Use gravity bombs

The most effective means of attacking a buried target, however, is to use a hard-cased earth-penetrating weapon which bores deep into the ground before exploding. The energy force of the explosion is transmitted very rapidly through the ground to the objective. The

Subsurface detonations such as this Plowshare Sedan shot on July 6, 1962, can destroy almost any conceivable target with less collateral damage than surface bursts. An earth-penetrating weapon has been considered for the B-2. USAF via Chuck Hansen

result is an underground "earthquake" or shock wave, which is twenty to fifty times as effective against a buried target as a surface detonation of the same yield. Even a small nuclear earth-penetrator, therefore, would be far more effective than the massive MK53.

Once again, missiles are of questionable use in delivering such attacks. ICBMs and SLBMs, paradoxically, are too fast. So much energy is released in the initial ground contact that it is almost impossible for the warhead mechanism to survive. The proposed solution to this problem is the EPMaRV (earth-penetrating, maneuvering RV), which sheds speed in a high-altitude maneuvering trajectory before diving on the target. EPMaRV, however, involves

some new technology in guidance and control. Cruise missiles, by contrast, are slow and low-flying, and may not be able to generate enough kinetic energy to deliver an earth-penetrating warhead without some form of boost—which, together with the earth-penetrating heavy shell, will cut into the missile's already limited payload.

The technology to put a gravity bomb up to 100 feet into moderately hard soil, however, has not only been developed but is more than forty years old. The Tallboy and Grand Slam conventional bombs developed in Britain during World War II could accomplish this from an altitude of 20,000 feet, impacting at about Mach 1.2. An earth-penetrating nuclear weapon, the Mk 8,

SAC bombers were used to drop conventional bombs in the Vietnam war; this B-52D is in the black and three-tone jungle camouflage used during that conflict. SAC has *developed improved tactics and weapons to allow its bombers, including the B-2, to be used more effectively in any future conventional war. Boeing*

was developed in the United States and briefly deployed in the fifties.

At the time of this writing, an earth-penetrating ICBM warhead is under development, but in view of budget cuts and the limited funds available for ICBM research, the bomber is still a strong candidate. In any case, the bomber's ability to deliver megaton-range warheads in laydown attacks gives it a greater hard-target capability than a conventionally tipped missile.

Another unique attribute of the bomber is its ability to inflict more damage at greater range with non-nuclear weapons than any other weapon, a capability which has been repeatedly cited in connection with the B-2 (although USAF Secretary Edward C. "Pete" Aldridge played it down at the B-2 roll-out).

Even non-nuclear earth-penetrating weapons, such as the 2,000 pound BLU-109, can cause immense damage to storage bunkers, hardened tactical missile sites, airfields and transport chokepoints, provided that they are delivered with sufficient accuracy. Bombers can deliver these weapons accurately and in large numbers. In some circumstances

—if, for example, a mission has to be carried out beyond fighter range from existing bases—they can also attack more quickly and with less warning than any other system.

Adding its low-observable characteristics and long range to this menu of survival techniques, the B-2 should be able not only to survive but to achieve an even higher level of surprise than current bombers. For example, it has been argued that one or two B-2s, operating from a base in the continental United States, could have delivered as many weapons on target as the El Dorado Canyon operation against Libya in April 1986, a mission which in fact took more than fifty fighters, back-ups, tankers and support aircraft.

But the B-2's primary mission is nuclear attack. The justification for its existence is that it can hit its targets with gravity bombs and short-range missiles, rather than launching cruise missiles from 1,500 miles away. In order to do this it must defeat the PVO, the Soviet Union's Troops of National Air Defense, operator of the world's biggest air defense system.

Chapter 6

Stealth tactics

Defense against the B-2 is not affordable.

General William Thurman, commander of USAF Aeronautical Systems Division, in January 1988

In every Western nation, air defense is just one of the air force's missions. Not so in the Soviet Union, where the PVO stands as an independent service dedicated to air and space defense, having no direct organizational connection with the other Soviet military aviation echelons. It generates its own requirements for fighters, missiles and support systems, which have tended to be different from those assigned to defend tactical targets. Two main divisions of the PVO

The Ilyushin Mainstay airborne early warning and control (AEW&C) aircraft is capable of tracking low-flying targets. Combined with its mobility, this extends the horizon of accurate radar coverage thousands of miles beyond the Soviet coastline. It is based on the Il-76 Candid military transport. US Department of Defense

concern us: the IA-PVO, which operates manned fighter aircraft, and the ZA-PVO, which is responsible for SAMs. Since the early sixties, the PVO has provided a deeply layered defense for Soviet strategic targets, exploiting the Soviet Union's vast land area to extend the defensive rim as far out as possible.

Soviet defense system

The first line of defense extends up to 1,000 miles from the outermost usable bases, well above the Arctic Circle. Its eyes are over-the-horizon radars, which have long range but relatively poor ability to track individual targets, forward-located surface-based radars and, increasingly, airborne radar systems. The first of these was the Tu-126 *Moss*, introduced in the late sixties. Although the system is unsophisticated, the aircraft has a long endurance and room for operators, relief crews and communications equipment. The Tu-126, however, is now being replaced by the Ilyushin *Mainstay* (its designation is unknown) which is much more advanced and can track low-flying targets

Apart from the large rotodome above the fuselage, the Mainstay features a satellite communications antenna ahead of the wing, passive electronic surveillance measures antennas on the sides of the nose and tail, and an inflight refueling probe. US Department of Defense

The primary long-range fighter in the Soviet air defense system is the MiG-31 Foxhound, 160 of which were in service by early 1988. It carries the largest radar of any fighter and four AA-9 Amos missiles, with a range as great as 100 miles. US Department of Defense

against ground clutter. Probably, too, its computers can maintain and display the tracks of many aircraft.

Long-range fighters

The "teeth" of the outer defense line are very large long-range fighters with no direct equivalent in the West. Because they are not designed to combat other fighters, they do not have to dogfight and have therefore been allowed to grow in range, weapon capability and size. In fact, the first such aircraft, the Tupolev Tu-28P *Fiddler*, was mistakenly classified as a bomber when it was first detected by the West. Armed with four very large air-to-air missiles, and equipped with a powerful radar, the Tu-28P probably had two missions. While its primary purpose was to destroy bombers, it would also acquire important data on the track, strength and disposition of an incoming bomber force which would be data-linked back to the PVO headquarters.

The Tu-28P is now being replaced by the Mikoyan MiG-31 *Foxhound*. The MiG-31 has been derived from the MiG-25 *Foxbat*—originally developed to shoot down the B-70—by stretching its body and adding a second cockpit. The missile stations are moved from the wings to the belly, and the wing hardpoints are occupied by large fuel tanks. It is not unlikely that the engines have been changed. Speed and climb performance are thus sacrificed in the interests of range. The MiG-31 is a "look-down, shoot-down" (LDSD) system which can engage low-flying targets.

The MiG-31 carries four AA-9 *Amos* missiles, virtual clones of the US AIM-54 Phoenix AAM (the missiles are very similar in length, diameter and configuration). Like Phoenix, the AA-9 is an "active-homing" missile with a miniature radar in its nose. While it is guided by the launch aircraft in the first stages of its flight, its radar will eventually detect the target and guide the missile to impact. Such missiles are lethal but tend to be expensive.

Short-range fighters

The next element of the layered PVO defense is formed by shorter-range

Capable of Mach 2.8, the MiG-25 Foxbat is a formidable interceptor despite its age. The original Foxbat-A fighters have been up- *graded to Foxbat-E variants, with a more versatile radar. US Department of Defense*

one-pilot fighters. Because of their range, these fighters defend a smaller zone of airspace around their base, and operate within the range of ground-based radar. The majority of the 2,200 plus fighters assigned to air defense of the Soviet Union fall into this category, and air defense zones cover the entire country. Before the early eighties, these aircraft were mostly under the control of the country's "military districts," but more recently central PVO control has been tightened.

Again, this echelon is being substantially modernized. The Sukhoi Su-15 and Su-21 *Flagon*, which are of antiquated concept, are being replaced by the Mikoyan MiG-29 *Fulcrum* and Sukhoi Su-27 *Flanker*. These elegant and formidable fighters are, if not brothers, certainly cousins. While they were designed by different teams (Soviet aircraft are planned and produced under central control, but designed and tested by independent bureaus) they share a common basic layout and carry similar weapons, in the shape of the large AA-10

AAM. Both have been designed to combat other fighters and tactical strike aircraft as well as bombers, in a departure from previous practice.

Parked near this MiG-25U Foxbat-C proficiency trainer is the multipurpose servicing vehicle which accompanies it on the flight line. Auxiliary power supplies, mobile test equipment and replenishables (such as oxygen) are combined on this vehicle, which also tows the fighter to the flight-line.

Sukhoi's predatory Su-27 Flanker-B is a dual-role fighter, designed both for tactical air superiority and strategic air defense. Bigger than the USAF's F-15, it is a single-seater with a very large "look-down" radar and an infrared search and track system.
US Department of Defense

Armament of the Su-27 includes a family of missiles with different capabilities, based on similar components. Here, medium-range, semi-active homing AA-10A missiles are carried on the centerline; medium-range infrared-homing AA-10B missiles are mounted on the wing pylons; and long-range, radar-homing AA-10C weapons, with a longer boost motor, are carried under the engine nacelles. US Department of Defense

Older fighters assigned to the air-defense role include the MiG-23 Flogger, armed with a pair of radar-guided AA-7s and a pair of infrared-homing AA-8 missiles. US Department of Defense

These zone-defense fighters operate with the aid of a "ground environment" including radar, computers and control systems. (It is possible that the Soviet Union's small early-warning radar aircraft, the Antonov *Madcap*, is designed as a "gap-filler" for the short-range surveillance network.) Finally, however, it is the fighter pilot's responsibility to locate and destroy the target.

SAMs

The PVO also maintains a very large force of SAMs to defend targets which are most likely to suffer bomber attack, such as air bases, command centers and industrial complexes. Long equipped with somewhat ancient systems such as the SA-1, SA-2 and SA-3, which were designed in the fifties to shoot down high-flying B-52s, the ZA-PVO now has an increasing number of SA-10 missile systems. Introduced in 1980, the SA-10 can handle multiple targets simultaneously; it uses phased-array, monopulse radars which are difficult to jam; and the missile has active homing, allowing it

to pursue a target which may be masked from its tracking and acquisition radars.

The PVO also operates two systems which fall between the classic definition of point and zone defense and which,

The massive SA-5 Griffon *missile was developed specifically to shoot down high-altitude, high-speed targets such as the B-58, B-70 and SR-71. It is now used in a tactical role, to threaten aircraft such as the E-3 AWACS.* US Department of Defense

The MiG-23 will eventually be replaced by the MiG-29, armed with the same AA-10 missiles as the Su-27, Like the Su-27, it can engage low-flying targets. US Department of Defense

like the MiG-31, have no direct equivalents in the West. The SA-5 missile and MiG-25 *Foxbat* fighter were designed to intercept the high-and-fast-flying B-70 and SR-71. The MiG-25 has an effective range of some 200 miles, and the missile has a maximum range of 150 miles.

SAMs can also be used to cover relocatable targets and fortified bunkers. While the effective range of most SAM systems is not great enough for area defense, the zone which they can defend is sufficiently large that the presence of a SAM radar does not provide an attacker with a useful clue as to the precise location of the target.

The assumption, sometimes made, that ICBMs and SLBMs will have wrecked

or crippled the air defense system long before the bombers arrive is probably incorrect. As noted in the previous chapter, the conflict may not start with a maximum-rate exchange of every available missile. Even so, a well-designed air defense system may survive an attack, and the PVO has had to face such a threat since the late fifties, when the USAF started development of thermonuclear counter-defense weapons (such as Hound Dog) for its bombers.

Many components of the Soviet air-defense system are mobile or relocatable. SAM launchers and radars can be moved from their normal sites to a concealed back-up bunker in a time of crisis; if the reserve site has never been used,

Soviet investment in SAMs has produced complex systems such as the SA-12B. A fielded system is mounted on tracked vehicles: two launchers (front, left and right), a reload transporter (front, center), a command vehicle (rear, center) and early-warning and tracking radars (rear, left and right). The system probably uses "track-via-missile" guidance, which is extremely difficult to jam. US Department of Defense

The mobile SA-10 system is replacing the older SA-1, SA-2 and SA-3 in service with the Soviet air defense forces. The missile is believed to carry an active seeker (a miniature radar) so that it can continue to engage a low-level target even if it becomes masked from the system's tracking radar. US Department of Defense

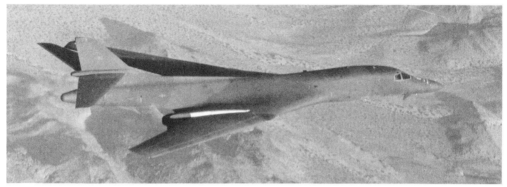

The B-1B relies for its survival on its ability to fly for long periods at low level, complicat- *ing fighter pursuit and screening it from most land-based radars.* Rockwell

the chances that its location will be known are slim.

Airfield trucks

Fighter airfields can certainly be hit, but the question is whether the fighters will be there. Western experts have noticed that every PVO fighter seems to be accompanied on the airfield by a large truck, which carries the same identifying tail number as the fighter. The truck is equipped to provide the fighter with electrical power, carry out basic diagnostic tests on its systems, pump fuel into its tanks, tow it to the flight-line and start its engines. The Soviet way of maintaining aircraft is also very different from Western philosophy, which emphasizes minimum cost per flying hour. All components of a Soviet aircraft are designed to function for a certain number of hours (roughly twice the hours that the aircraft would be expected to operate in wartime), after which they are removed from the aircraft and returned to a depot for overhaul. The idea is that the commander starts the war with, on average, enough time-before-overhaul left on all his weap-

ons and systems to get through the conflict without major maintenance.

Putting these two points together, it is clear that the PVO fighter force is designed so that the fighters can leave their normal bases in wartime and operate from civilian airports, specially strengthened roads or abandoned military bases, with support provided by their consort trucks. Because they require only "line" maintenance, the absence of main-base facilities is of little importance. Overall, therefore, the PVO is in good shape to weather an attack.

The successive layers of the PVO system are designed to reduce the numbers of attackers at each stage, while acquiring an increasing amount of information on the locations and tracks of the survivors. The system is far larger and better equipped than the wartime Luftwaffe at its best, and the numbers of attackers much smaller.

Penetration strategy

SAC, however, has consistently maintained that it can penetrate the system to a depth of 2,000 miles or more and strike its assigned targets, through a combination of equipment, tactics and skill.

The foundation of modern bomber tactics is that the bomber flies alone. Any advantage to be gained from mutual support is overwhelmed by the greater risk of detection and identification, and by the possibility that all aircraft in a group may be lost if they are engaged by fighters or a SAM system. Formation or group tactics also imply communication and the risk of betraying location through radio signals.

On the other hand, this does not rule out the coordination of bomber

Bristling with antennas, this Lockheed U-2R is used by SAC to intercept radar signals and communications traffic. SIGINT (signals intelligence) is vital to the task of mapping Soviet air defenses and determining how they would operate in wartime. Lockheed

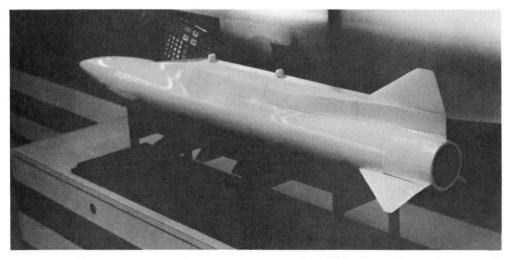

Boeing's AGM-131 SRAM II (short-range attack missile) is a rocket-boosted nuclear bomb with an inertial guidance system. Its range is dependent on launch altitude, exceeding 200 miles under optimum conditions. Its ogival nose and faceted dorsal spine minimize its RCS.

ingress routes, in space and time, in order to put the defenses to as much trouble as possible. The key is to keep the bombers close together in time but separated in space. Thus, the defending commander has little time to deal with the targets before they reach the next zone, and his controllers are overtaxed. At the same time, however, the bombers are crossing his perimeter hundreds of miles apart, so that his fighters are limited, by their speed and their range, in their ability to go from one engagement point to another.

The same philosophy can apply to countering SAMs, the difference being that the spatial separation between the bombers is best expressed in terms of the compass rather than the map. Few SAM systems can engage targets simultaneously in diametrically different directions without operating at much less than their peak efficiency.

Route planning starts with a list of targets to be attacked and the weapons available. The power of thermonuclear gravity weapons means that few if any targets need to be hit more than once. The B-2 can carry sixteen nuclear weapons, but it is unlikely that a B-2 would be able to deliver that many separate gravity-bomb attacks in a single mission and survive. Instead, SAC penetrators carry a mix of bombs and missiles, which are less accurate, but can be launched from outside the range of SAMs which surround the target.

Offensive weapons

The B-2's primary weapons will be the Boeing AGM-131A SRAM II missile and the B83 bomb. The SRAM (short-range attack missile) II is a direct replacement for the original Boeing AGM-69 SRAM, which was designed in the sixties and is now growing old and diffi-

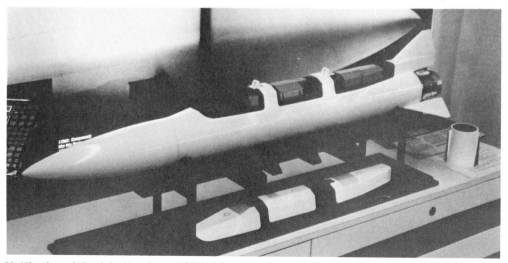

Unlike the original, bullet-shaped SRAM, the new SRAM II is logically laid out, with easily accessible avionics in the dorsal spine. It is roughly the same size and weight as the B83 nuclear bomb.

A test model of the B83 bomb is released from an F-111. Much of the bomb's volume is taken up by the parachute system, which must decelerate the weapon very rapidly if it is to survive a "laydown" delivery. Sandia National Laboratory via Chuck Hansen

cult to maintain. It is not a complicated weapon, consisting of a 200 kiloton warhead, a rocket motor and a Litton laser-gyro inertial navigation system. The range of the original SRAM varied according to its launch altitude, from fifty miles at sea level to 200 miles at high altitude. The performance of the SRAM II is classified but is claimed to be better. The SRAM II is accurate, because it is highly supersonic and its range is relatively short—inertial navigation systems drift with time, not distance. While the SRAM was originally designed to destroy missile sites and radar installations in the bomber's path, it is now regarded as a primary weapon against relatively soft, relocatable targets. It is due to enter service in 1993.

The B83 is described by the USAF as a "gravity weapon" because it is unguided and unpowered. It is the newest type of strategic nuclear bomb developed for the USAF, and was designed by the Department of Energy's Lawrence Livermore Nuclear Laboratory in California. It has a selectable yield between one and two megatons, and is the first production bomb to be designed for "laydown" delivery against hard, irregular targets. In such a delivery, the bomb is delay-fused so that the bomber can escape to a safe distance before the explosion. In contrast to airburst or contact fusing, however, this means that the bomb must survive the initial impact with the ground, and land without bouncing or rolling.

The bombers will each be assigned several targets. Some will be destroyed before they reach all or any of their targets, so each target is also assigned to more than one bomber; the highest-priority, most heavily defended objectives may be the targets for several bombers. The bomber crew are expected to assess damage. If the first penetrator is destroyed and the second hits the target, the crew of the third will observe that the target has been destroyed and proceed to their next objective. Many variations on this theme are possible: one bomber's primary target may be another's secondary, and there is no reason why one bomber should not be assigned to primary, secondary, tertiary or even more targets, provided that the resulting route does not exceed its range and can be covered with a reasonable chance of survival. Additionally, targets can be allocated to the bomber's SRAM missiles, up to 100 miles away from its track.

Navigation and targeting

The key to finding the target is the same as it has been since the days of the Zeppelin: look in the right place. The bomber that cruises around searching randomly for its objective is setting itself up for a fighter attack, giving away the mobility and unpredictability which are its best hope for survival. Accurate navigation is therefore critical.

The B-2's inertial navigation system (INS) was developed by the Kearfott Guidance and Navigation Corporation, which produced the INS for the B-1. INS was originally developed for bombers, but is now used on many military and commercial aircraft. It measures every acceleration and deceleration of the aircraft in three dimensions, and extrapolates speed, track and position from a known starting point. Until the late seventies, INS units were complex devices based on mechanical gyroscopes, and were costly to maintain. The B-2, however, probably uses a solid-state INS in which the whirling masses of metal are replaced by ring laser gyros (RLG, laser beams traveling on a track through a square or triangular glass block). Originally, RLG systems were less accurate than the highly sophisticated electro-mechanical INS used on bombers, but technological improvements have changed the picture. An important advantage of a change to RLG technology on the B-2 is that it could carry two or three inertial platforms to guard against failure.

Some of the B-2's targets may be mobile, and their positions may not be precisely known. The bomber crew's latest information may be freshly transmitted via Milstar, or it may be hours or days old. Even in the latter case, the bomber crew do not have to search completely at random. SS-24 missiles will not move off rail tracks, and SS-25s will not move far off roads. Neither is likely to be emplaced in the middle of an empty, rolling steppe. Mobile command centers must transmit in order to do their job, or stay close to established land-lines.

Radar

The B-2's radar, developed by the Radar Systems Group of Hughes Aircraft (part of General Motors), is its most important tool for finding imprecisely located or relocatable targets. A criticism which has been leveled at the concept of a low-observable bomber is that it will have no way of finding its targets at long standoff ranges without betraying its presence by radar emissions. This argument may be a measure of the effectiveness of the security which

has protected the development of low-probability-of-intercept (LPI) radar technology over many years. Most LPI techniques are classified, but are likely to include the adaptive management of power (the radar gradually increases its power until it can see a target, and then holds its power level), the use of very-low-sidelobe antennas, and constant variations in frequency and waveform. The same fundamental fact that underlies the potential of LPI applies also to Stealth. Because people have tended to assume as a matter of course that any radar transmission will be intercepted and classified, there was enormous room for improvement in terms of LPI.

The B-2 radar has two antennas built into the lower leading edge of the wing, one on each side. Rather than moving physically, they are probably scanned electronically to steer the radar beam. From the B-2's cruising altitude, the radar can scan at least a 150 mile swath of ground with minimal shadowing effects. Hughes' earlier ASARS-2 reconnaissance radar, which is about the same size as the B-2 system, has been described as "producing a picture of the battlefield" at a range of 100 miles when fitted to the TR-1.

Low RCS

Navigation and targeting are one of the two main elements of the bomber's mission; the other is survival. The first basic rule is to go where the defenses are weakest. Each radar has its own characteristic detection envelope, or a volume within which it will probably detect a target of a given size. It depends on its effective power, its antenna size and shape and its location. Knowing where the radars are located is vital, so SAC maintains a large fleet of aircraft devoted to electronic reconnaissance.

Because of the B-2's Stealth design, the area covered by an individual radar shrinks considerably, and what was once an interlinked defensive chain may be full of gaps that the bombers can exploit. Even if a radar picks up a B-2, the defenders will have less time to react before the bomber leaves the radar's area of coverage.

The Soviet Union has invested far more resources in SAM systems than the West; these systems, however, are severely degraded by Stealth. Medium-range and long-range SAMs rely on radar from target acquisition to the point where the warhead detonates. A SAM system includes search and tracking radars which are matched in performance to the missile; but this assumes a certain value for target RCS. Against a

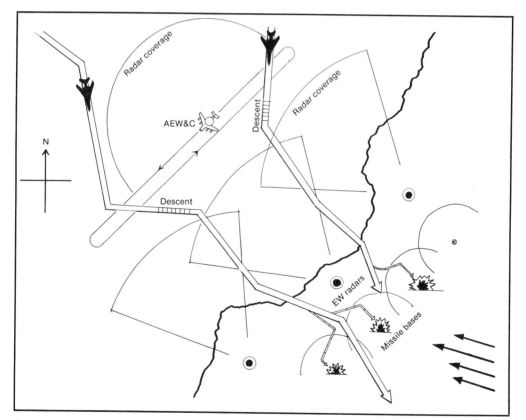

Contemporary bomber tactics: bombers approaching from the northwest cannot avoid detection by airborne warning and control (AEW&C) aircraft or an overlapping chain of ground-based EW radars. By changing course and dropping to low altitude, they can delay detection, but the chain of missile sites will nevertheless be pre-warned. While the missile sites can be attacked with SRAM missiles, the fighters approaching from the southeast cannot be so readily countered, and some of the bombers will be lost.

low-RCS target, the system becomes mismatched. The search radar cannot detect the target in time to hand it to the tracking and illumination radar, and the tracker cannot track the target until it is almost inside the system's minimum range.

An animated map of a planned bomber attack would be likely to show dozens of tracks lighting up simultaneously along the maximum range of the defenses' detection systems. As the attack develops, the tracks snake through valleys, over saddles, and on the shadow side of ridges; they wind around some SAM sites and cross over others. Some tracks feint in one direction, vanish into a radar shadow and emerge on a different bearing.

Visual detection

Night and bad weather are the bomber's allies. The crews of earlier bombers were almost blind in the visual spectrum. Before crossing into hostile

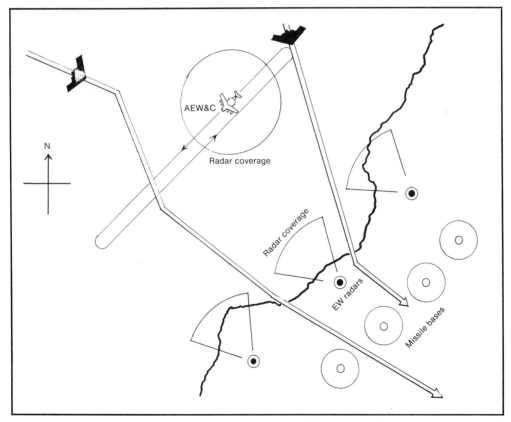

B-2 tactics: a sharp cut in radar detection range makes the AEW&C aircraft much easier to evade, and opens up gaps in the coverage of ground-based radars, even at high level. With no early warning, and with targets at their maximum effective range, SAMs are unable to engage the bombers effectively.

territory, the crew would fit metal covers over the windshields to protect their eyesight from the blinding flashes of nuclear explosions. Their outside view was restricted to a pair of small portholes made of a photoreactive crystal material called PZLT, which darkens almost instantaneously in response to bright light. The B-2 has a less constricting defense against flash. A photosensitive coating on the windshield protects the cockpit interior, and the crew wear PZLT goggles. (This should also protect the crew from high-powered lasers.) Darkness or cloud can only make it more difficult for a fighter to find the bomber, without impeding the bomber's ability to navigate or find its targets.

Some factors favor the bomber crew despite the vast numerical superiority of the defensive force. One is the radar-range equation, which ensures that the bomber's electronic warfare system will receive signals from hostile radars long before the bomber is detected. A commonly used analogy is that of a band of men with flashlights, stalking a lone quarry in open ground on a moonless night. Who will see whom first? This factor will become far more important with the arrival of the B-2; its electronic warfare systems will be able to detect, pinpoint and identify hostile emitters with a considerable degree of confidence before they can track it.

Planned routes and actual routes are unlikely to be the same. While the route is planned to reduce the probability of detection, that is all that it can do. Sometimes a bomber will fly brazenly past a radar which is temporarily out of commission and get clean away. Sometimes, a radar crew will secure an accu-

B-2 crews will wear light-sensitive PZLT goggles to protect their eyesight from nuclear flash, while a photoreactive layer in the cockpit windows will protect the equipment inside the cockpit. Currently, B-1 crews have to install rigid screens over the windshield, restricting their vision to small PZLT portholes. Boeing

rate position as the bomber pops up briefly from concealment. Or, a radar's position may not have been accurately known to the route planner. Fighters and airborne radars, of course, can appear almost anywhere.

Speed

Fighters are dangerous, but suffer from one limitation: while a bomber is not as fast as a fighter, the speeds which the two types of aircraft can sustain, for much more than five minutes, are similar. Both operate normally at speeds around 500 to 600 mph. A fighter such as the MiG-29 may be able to fly at twice this speed, but only by using full augmented thrust and burning fuel at an enormous rate.

If the bomber can avoid continuous radar tracking, a pursuing fighter will be vectored to the bomber's projected location, based on its speed and track the last time the ground controller picked it up, rather than an actual location. But the controller and the fighter pilot must appreciate that the bomber's crew were probably well aware that they were being watched, and may have feinted onto a different track before leaving the radar's search envelope and jinking back to their original course. The bomber's actual location and its projected position (that is, where the pilot and the controller think it is) may be diverging at several miles per minute. The bomber may be anywhere within a rapidly expanding area of uncertainty.

The fighter pilot can, of course, shrink the circle of uncertainty by using augmented power and dashing to the bomber's projected position at supersonic speed. Even if the bomber has feinted, it will not have had time to move very far from its last position. But if this tactic fails and the fighter pilot fails to locate the bomber within minutes, he is out of the fight. Although the fighter is still in one piece, the bomber has achieved a "mission kill" by forcing it to return to base.

A similar situation applies in the case of airborne warning and control (AEW&C) aircraft such as the *Moss* or the *Mainstay*. These expensive aircraft are scarce in any air force, and usually patrol in carefully coordinated (and hence predictable) "racetrack" patterns to make the most of their radar coverage. Cruising at least as fast as the AEW&C aircraft, and warned of their presence at a vast distance by the characteristic signals from their radars, the bomber's crew can execute a dog-leg to avoid them. The principle is the same as waiting until the sentry has reached the other end of his beat before trying to scale the fence. Even if the B-2 is not as fast as the B-1, its ability to outfox the AEW&C aircraft will still be superior because the radar's range will be drastically reduced.

If the B-2 is ever used for conventional bombing missions, other tactical variations might be used. In the past, SAC has tended to hold its first-line bombers out of conventional missions; the losses suffered by its B-52 formations over North Vietnam may be a reason. Now, however, SAC considers that bombers can carry out conventional attacks without unacceptable losses, given appropriate targets and tactics. Essentially, the bombers would exploit their great range to attack targets in rear areas, where local defenses are thinner than at the forward edge of the battle area, and to approach these targets by indirect low-level routes. SAC crews are now practicing attacks in which several bombers arrive at the same target, on different routes and from different directions, at almost exactly the same time. This is diametrically opposed to the tactics used in Vietnam, where the bombers arrived at the target many minutes apart from the same direction. "We don't intend to do dumb things like that again," one officer commented.

Defensive weapons

While the B-2 has no tail guns, that is not to say that it has no defensive armament. SRAM II missiles can either be used against pre-assigned targets or against emitters which are located on the way into the target. However, automated EW will be the last line of defense if the B-2 needs to venture into close proximity of a SAM radar or is tracked by a fighter.

Electronic jamming and the use of decoys, chaff and flares are next-to-last-ditch measures even though they are essential. The risk, with any sort of jamming, is that the emitted power which jams one threat may alert another, one of the most serious problems with the B-1B's electronic warfare system.

Little is known of the B-2's EW suite, which includes components from Raytheon, Sanders Associates and Honeywell, but it will be very different from that of the B-1. For one thing, it will require much less power. Almost any jammer ceases to operate when the radar receives the target's real reflection more strongly than the false signal or noise transmitted by the jammer (called "burn-through"). Obviously, the burn-through range varies with the target's reflectivity or RCS, the jammer's power and the jammer's ability to concentrate that power. It is less obvious, but a matter of mathematics and geometry, that burn-through range declines much more rapidly with RCS than the detection range, so that a Stealthy target can use jamming much more effectively than a non-Stealthy aircraft. The benefits can be taken in many ways. It can jam with less power, producing a lighter, simpler system which is less likely to alert an enemy; or it can use any of a number of EW techniques which can be made to work efficiently on small targets, but not on large ones.

Crew

Navigation, route planning, target search, defense evasion and suppres-

sion and jamming are no small major task for the four-man crew of the B-1. The B-2, however, will be flown by two men, with provision for a third. This should have come as less of a surprise than it did, in some ways. At the time the B-1 was designed, after all, long-range jetliner crews were only just shrinking from four people to three, and the latest 747-400 and MD-11 will be flown by two pilots.

The B-2 follows this trend, using the same methods as the jetliners. In the B-2 cockpit, hundreds of single-purpose gauges, lights and switches will be replaced by eight large-format, computer-driven cathode-ray tube (CRT) displays provided by Allied-Signal. As well as replacing conventional flight and engine instruments, these displays can show anything which can be generated on board the aircraft. Printed flight manuals and system manuals are, in normal use, replaced by computer graphics on the CRTs. In the case of a hydraulic problem, for example, the CRT will display a diagram of the affected system; if the pilot shuts off a valve, the same valve will close on the CRT.

In combat, the B-2's information management system should be able to fuse data from many sources. Radar imagery, for example, will be superimposed on maps of the target area, acquired by satellite and stored on board the B-2. (One of the contractors in the B-2 program is Miltope, which specializes in high-density digital and optical disk drives for military applications.) The physical and electronic characteristics of known threats can also be stored and fused. If an SA-5 radar is detected, the system can display its location, its predicted area of coverage and the bomber's projected track on the CRT; the crew can determine instantly whether a course change is necessary.

Workload will be high in any event, and the B-2's range will make for twenty-hour missions. Training, as always in SAC, will be intensive. It is no coincidence that Link Flight Simulation Corporation is regarded as "a major subcontractor" on the B-2 team. High-tech simulators will enable B-2 crews to train against a wide range of realistic threats without leaving the ground. Indeed, SAC crews had "flown" the B-2 for hundreds of hours, on simulators, before the real aircraft was completed.

Anti-Stealth measures

There is little question that the B-2 will be effective against the defenses which the Soviet Union currently deploys; even the B-1 would be hard to catch despite the troubles of its EW system. Each new SAC bomber, however, has spurred improvements to the PVO's equipment. USAF officers, however, have claimed that defense against the B-2 is "not affordable."

Assessing the validity of this claim is impossible in the absence of figures on the B-2's radar cross section and other signatures, data which is likely to remain classified for many years to come. However, many ways in which radar, in particular, can be made more effective against targets of low RCS have been discussed. Some of them, at least, will have to be explored in the United States now that the low-RCS AS-15 Kent cruise missile has been deployed.

Stealth has not made radar obsolete, but it has certainly slowed, probably stopped and possibly reversed the trend toward better radar performance which accompanied improvements in electronics. But a number of basic counter-Stealth techniques have already been identified, launching a new phase in the electronic war. One of them, at least, threatens to neutralize known forms of radar-absorbent material (RAM).

LDSD

Some criticisms of the B-2 have been rooted in a misperception about look-down, shoot-down (LDSD) radar and missile systems. A look-down radar does not look down vertically, but at an oblique angle. It receives an echo from the target and a much stronger echo from the ground behind the target. A specially designed, high-speed computer discriminates between the target and ground echoes on the basis of the Doppler shift (the change in perceived frequency caused when the source of the signal is moving relative to the observer or receiver). The echo from the target, moving over the ground, has a different Doppler shift from the ground echo. The Doppler shift is strongest on the vector on which the target and the radar platform are moving (straight ahead) and becomes weaker as the vector from the target to the aircraft approaches ninety degrees. A vertical look-down radar—such as a space-based radar—would require fundamentally different technology.

LDSD also requires a great deal of processing power under ideal conditions. It requires a strong radar return, and the range of a radar in look-down is invariably less than its range against a high-flying target. Moreover, LDSD had not been tested in action by late 1988. To regard it as a particularly potent anti-

Stealth weapon is to exaggerate its potential.

SBR

The idea of using space-based radar (SBR) to detect the B-2 has also been mooted, as a result of the B-2's large planform area. However, there are problems with such a system that have yet to be resolved. It must detect targets at long range (its orbit is at least ninety miles above its targets) which requires a lot of power or a big antenna. It has to detect targets in a short period of time, before it moves out of range. It will also suffer from ground clutter against targets below 10,000 feet. This would give it a difficult task against any aircraft, and the B-2 is likely to be harder to detect, even in the vertical aspect, than conventional types.

Long-wavelength radar

One anti-Stealth measure is to increase the wavelength of the radar, and some sources have suggested that the long-wavelength early-warning radars in service in the Soviet Union, many of them dating back to the fifties, will easily detect the B-2. However, this is an oversimplification.

The effectiveness of long wavelengths against low-RCS targets rests on resonance effects between direct reflection from the target and waves which "creep" around it. Resonance occurs from components as well as from the whole aircraft. A gun muzzle may be resonant even when illuminated by an X-band fighter radar with a 3 cm wavelength. The Grumman E-2, with a radar operating at 400 MHz in the UHF band, puts out a 75 cm wave, so that quite large components (fin or wingtips, or the cross section of a missile body) may

fall within the resonance region. (Grumman has claimed that the E-2's General Electric radar, which has a longer wavelength than the radar fitted to the Boeing E-2 AWACS, is better able to detect small targets.)

The Soviet Union's older early-warning radars operate in the VHF band. Some of these are mobile, such as the *Spoon Rest* associated with the SA-4 and SA-2. Others, like the very large *Tall King*, are fixed and are used for strategic air and missile defense. (These strange names are assigned by NATO;

Part of the huge electronic array required by an over-the-horizon (OTH) antenna. OTH radars are capable of detecting very small targets, but without sufficient accuracy to track them or designate them for attack. General Electric

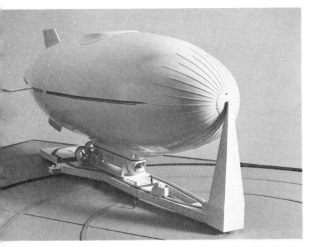

Westinghouse and Britain's Airship Industries are jointly building an experimental AEW&C airship for the US Navy. Its helium-filled envelope is 423 feet long and 136 feet in diameter, and will house a very large radar antenna. In fact, an airship can carry a larger, more sensitive radar antenna than almost any other mobile platform. The Navy airship is being studied as a way of protecting the fleet from future Stealthy cruise missiles. Westinghouse

Another way of providing a large radar aperture is to use a physically fixed, electronically steered "active array." This Fairchild Metro will be used by the Royal Swedish Air Force to test the Ericsson PS-90 radar, which may form the basis of a "mini-AWACS" in the nineties. Fairchild

some are related to the size and shape of the radar, while others, such as *Owl Screech*, reflect the characteristic electronic noise which the radar emits.) Precise frequencies vary, but *Tall King* is fairly typical at 160 to 180 MHz, with wavelengths of 165 to 190 cm. At this point, major components of large aircraft, such as wings and fins, may be resonant.

Over-the-horizon (OTH) radars invariably operate in the HF band with frequencies around 10 MHz and wavelengths of 30 m, because the OTH radar is confined to the band in which atmospheric reflection is effective. At that point, any target will generate some kind of resonance and shaping will be largely irrelevant to the size of the target's radar image.

The Stealth designer's answer to resonance is to eliminate smaller components from the shape, driving up the wavelengths at which resonance is likely to occur. The ultimate expression of this philosophy, not surprisingly, is a flying wing, in which the smallest dimension is measured in tens of feet.

However, increasing the wavelength of a radar is not simply a matter of turning a dial. The price of increasing wavelength, for the radar designer, is that the size of the antenna (its "aperture") has to grow in proportion to the wavelength in order to maintain a narrow beam and adequate resolution. The "mobile" Soviet VHF radars are cumbersome, and early-warning radars such as *Tall King* are large fixed structures and provide coverage of only one sector. OTH radars are larger still, extending over miles of the landscape.

Another problem with VHF and, to some extent, UHF radars is that those wavebands are stuffed with communications traffic. In the tactical environment, this generates so much noise that the ability of such radars to detect anything, let alone a Stealth aircraft, is reduced. This is why most such radars are found in the early-warning role, looking out over empty territory, rather than in tactical applications.

Developing airborne radars with long wavelengths requires a radical change to the design of the whole system. While it would presumably be possible to base an AWACS follow-on on a large aircraft such as the 747 or the Antonov An-124, with a larger rotodome than current systems, the cost would be great and the gain in performance would be marginal. Two approaches to the problem have been proposed; one relies on advanced electronic technology and the other is a throwback to an almost vanished era of aviation.

The latter is the US Navy's plan to demonstrate an AEW&C airship. In 1987, the Navy awarded a contract to Westinghouse and Airship Industries, a British company, to build a prototype airship with an extremely large radar antenna inside its envelope. Even a small airship can carry aloft a far larger antenna than any fixed-wing aircraft.

The high-tech approach is to use the modern technology of electronically steered radar antennas. Because these antennas do not have to move in order to steer their beams, it is possible to build wide-aperture arrays which are compatible with small aircraft. Interestingly, the furthest advanced program of this kind is being carried out in Sweden,

where a Fairchild Metro commuter aircraft is being fitted with a large Ericsson active-array radar antenna mounted above its fuselage. The aperture of this radar is similar to that of the AWACS radar, but it is carried on a 14,000 pound turboprop airplane rather than a 335,000 pound jet. A bigger airplane could carry a very large active array: the USAF has tested a mock-up of a sixty-foot antenna on a C-130. Future active arrays—consisting of many small transmitter/receiver modules—could be built into the wings and tail of an aircraft for 360 degree coverage, according to engineers at Grumman and General Electric who have been studying "conformal arrays" under contract to the USAF and Navy.

If active-array technology permits the installation of an AWACS-sized antenna on an aircraft the size of the Metro, it can clearly be used to put a much larger radar on a bigger platform. This is a wind-tunnel model of a 45-foot-long antenna developed by Lockheed, mounted on the side of a C-130. Lockheed

It is likely that the follow-ons to systems such as the USAF's AWACS and the Soviet *Mainstay* will use active arrays of very wide aperture. It is also certain that they will be expensive and difficult to develop. Even Sweden's active-array AEW radar, with relatively modest performance goals, is unlikely to be operational much before 1995, even though it has been under development for several years.

Bistatic radar

Another potential anti-Stealth technique is the use of bistatic radar, in which the transmitter and receiver are in different places. If a Stealth aircraft's shape is designed to deflect received radiation away from its source, it may still send a main lobe echo in another direction, to be picked up in full strength by a bistatic radar.

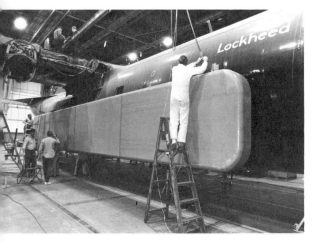

The size of the Lockheed active-array antenna is apparent in this view. Such systems contain thousands of small transmit/receive modules, each working in the same way as the single transmitter/receiver of a conventional radar. They are extremely powerful and very expensive. Lockheed

With a bistatic radar, the transmitter, the target and the receiver are at three corners of a triangle. A target can be located as long as the positions of the transmitter and receiver are known and the two are precisely synchronized. (Both these conditions can be inexpensively satisfied by the use of the satellite-based Navstar Global Positioning System or its equivalent.)

The bistatic radar can only detect a target which is in the area where the transmitter beam crosses the aspect covered by the receiving antenna. Searching a large area takes a relatively long time; one solution, the use of multiple antenna-receiver sets pointing in different directions, is cumbersome and expensive. Another approach to this problem is to use a wide-angle antenna known as a Rotman lens, in which a large mass of dielectric material refracts the incoming signal onto one of a series of ports, according to its arrival angle. By "jumping" the receiver over the ports in sequence, the bistatic radar can actually track the transmitter pulse as it proceeds out from the radar. This operation is known as "pulse chasing" and allows the receiver to detect any target in the illuminating beam and determine its bearing.

Bistatic radar's potential against Stealth targets tends as a matter of course to be a sensitive area. The normal concept of RCS is monostatic, and may not apply at all. Some shaping techniques, intended to deflect the main lobe of a radar return away from the transmitter, may under certain circumstances deflect it toward a bistatic receiver. Also, a bistatic receiver may intercept forward-scattered waves which are not suppressed by radar-absorbent material (RAM). However, notes one engineer, "the geometry has to be just right, and you can't always count on it." As a result, the main benefit of bistatic radar may be its relative immunity from anti-radar attack rather than its anti-Stealth qualities.

Carrier-free radar

In late 1986, however, a third way of countering Stealth technology by radar was publicized in the electrical engineering press. While it is little more than a theoretical concept backed up by laboratory data (at least in the United States) it has so much potential that it has been dubbed the "anti-Stealth radar" in some circles.

RAM dissipates radar energy by the re-alignment of loose electrons under the influence of the high-frequency radar wave. But if the radar pulses have no dominant carrier frequency, but instead approximate to a "square" pulse of radar energy, this absorption mechanism does not exist. Radars which generate such pulses already exist. Called "carrier-free" radars, they are used, among other things, for imaging the interiors of sealed concrete structures.

According to electrical engineers familiar with this technology, the main challenges involved in developing an "anti-Stealth" surveillance radar, the design of the transmitter and receiver, are straightforward technical problems—albeit very large ones. One engineer sums them up as "catching up on the countless millions of dollars which have been spent on sinusoidal radar over the years."

In the United States, work on carrier-free radar has been on a very small scale, mainly because its potential use against Stealth targets went virtually unrecognized until 1985. What little work is under way appears to be classified, and there does not seem to be a program to develop a full-scale radar yet. But wishing will not make the carrier-free radar go away. The subject has received some attention in the Soviet Union and China, and technical papers published in China suggest that engineers in that country may already have produced an experimental transmitter and receiver.

The B-2 is not invisible, and a means will eventually be found to detect it. It is not an "ultimate" weapon, and there will never be any such thing. But if it performs as it is supposed to perform, it may be survivable for a longer period than its critics assume. The Soviet air defense system has 7,000 radars. If the Soviet Union developed a more effective type of radar today, and managed to deploy the first by the B-2's IOC date in 1994, and began to retrofit all its missile sites at the rate of five per week—all wildly optimistic assumptions, from the Soviet viewpoint—it would complete the program in 2021.

It may be true that defense against the B-2 is not affordable. The same, increasingly, is being said of the B-2 itself; if the Northrop bomber is built in quantity, there can be little doubt that it will be the last US strategic bomber built in our working lifetimes. Total war seems on the point of becoming a luxury that the world cannot afford.

Other Stealth programs

The uncompromising secrecy surrounding the B-2 and other Stealth programs may or may not have obstructed foreign efforts to acquire such technology, but it has certainly confused most Americans. The ATB is sometimes called the "Stealth," a generic term that applies equally to several other programs. The

The USAF's Advanced Tactical Fighter will use its Stealth characteristics to remain undetected by hostile fighters until it has fired its own missiles. Lockheed

name "Stealth fighter" can also be applied to more than one program, leading to further confusion. Combined with the virtual extinction of aerospace literacy within the US mass media, these terminological inexactitudes have muddied the picture beyond the wildest hopes of any Pentagon disinformation specialist.

The term "Stealth warplane" is in fact becoming a tautology in the United States. The McDonnell Douglas C-17 will probably be the last US aircraft, among those designed for use in proximity to an armed opponent, which does not reflect Stealth technology in its basic design. In addition to the B-2 and the Lockheed F-117, the following Stealth programs are under way.

McDonnell Douglas/ General Dynamics A-12

The A-12, the US Navy's Advanced Tactical Aircraft (ATA), has been developed in much the same secrecy as the B-2. The program's schedule and budgets, for example, are classified. A McDonnell Douglas/General Dynamics team was chosen to develop the A-12 late in 1987, in preference to a Northrop/Grumman/Vought group, after a competitive demonstration and validation effort. This accords with earlier Navy statements that the program is two years ahead of the USAF's ATF, which implied an initial operating capability (IOC) in 1993-94. The A-12 is designed to replace the A-6 Intruder, and has been characterized as a long-range, heavy-payload Stealth aircraft. It is powered by two GE F404-F5D2 engines. Norden and Texas Instruments are developing its radar, its central computer is from IBM and its electro-optical subsystem is being developed by Westinghouse. Around 300 aircraft will be required by the US Navy. Under an agreement signed in 1986, the US Air Force will consider the A-12 for any future long-range strike requirements, such as a replacement for the F-111.

USAF Advanced Tactical Fighter

The importance of Stealth in the ATF requirement was greatly increased during the definition stage, and probably led to the selection of Stealth pioneers as the prime contractors for the competitive demo-val stage which is now under way. Lockheed, Boeing and General Dynamics are developing the YF-22, and Northrop and McDonnell Douglas are producing the YF-23. Two prototypes of each are due to fly in early 1990; one aircraft of each type will fly with the Pratt & Whitney F119, and the other with GE's F120. The current schedule calls for the USAF to select one of the designs in 1991 and for IOC in 1995, although this may be delayed to save money in the early years of the decade. The ATF is expected to have a radar cross section at least 100 times smaller than current fighters, allowing it to penetrate even Central Region air defenses with a minimal risk of detection. The USAF plans to replace the F-15 with 750 ATFs. Under the same agreement that covers the A-12, the Navy views the ATF, in theory, as the replacement for the F-14.

General Dynamics AGM-129 Advanced Cruise Missile

General Dynamics was selected to produce the ACM strategic cruise missile in 1983 after problems emerged with a "black" Lockheed weapon. ACM will, initially, arm B-52H bombers of the 410th Bomb Wing at K. I. Sawyer AFB in Michigan. When SAC's B-1Bs are replaced in the penetration role by B-2s, they will be equipped with ACMs. The ACM is not only more Stealthy than the current ALCM, but is also more powerful (allowing it to follow terrain more closely) and has a greater range. The missile was originally intended to become operational in 1989-90, but the program is understood to have encountered problems and this date may not be met.

In addition to these programs, it is considered more than likely that the USAF is developing some form of Stealth aircraft for the reconnaissance role. *The New York Times* reported in early 1988 that a Stealth strategic surveillance aircraft capable of Mach 5 cruising speeds was under development. Whether this is the case or not, Stealth makes a great deal of sense for such missions.

The Flying Wing controversy

The rediscovery of the flying wing was particularly important to Northrop, because the history of the original versions is one of the most controversial stories in aviation, to this day, and was a tremendously important and ultimately tragic chapter in Northrop's existence.

Jack Northrop was one of a small group of Californian engineers who, between 1925 and 1935, revolutionized the technology of transport aircraft and doubled the speed of air travel. Biplanes, festooned with struts and wires, gave way to monoplanes. Landing gear was made retractable. Engines were encased in streamlined cowlings, reducing drag and providing better cooling at the same time. Boxy shapes of steel tube skinned with fabric or corrugated metal gave way to light, strong, smooth shapes formed of thin aluminum skins with internal stiffeners and bulkheads. Northrop was particularly noted for his work on structures, and his "multi-cellular" structural design formed the basis of the apparently everlasting Douglas DC-3.

Jack Northrop saw such designs as steps toward the ultimate all-wing aircraft, in which the drag of the body and the tail would be eliminated. After demonstrating a privately funded prototype, the N-1M, to the USAAF, Northrop won support for his ideas and a contract to develop the XB-35 bomber, a giant for its day.

Unfortunately, Northrop could never prove his claims of superior range performance. The XB-35 was plagued by problems with the propeller gearboxes,

The N-9M was designed as a one-third-scale model of the XB-35. Four such aircraft were built, and they were invaluable in the devel- opment of the bomber's unique control system. Northrop

and could not demonstrate its estimated performance. The USAF was eager to acquire an intercontinental bomber and preferred the bigger, more complex but more conventional Convair B-36. A year before the XB-35 flew in June 1946, the USAF had decided to complete the third and fourth aircraft of the type with jets, as YB-49s. They would be faster but would not be able to match the range of the B-36.

The jet-powered YB-49 flew in October 1947. While it did not equal the range of the XB-35, it had a greater range than any other jet bomber, and only Boeing's XB-47 was faster. In June 1948, the second YB-49 crashed on a flight from the US Air Force's flight-test center at Muroc AFB, in the high desert above Los Angeles. All on board were killed, and Muroc was later renamed in honor of the aircraft commander, Captain Glen Edwards. The cause of the accident was never established beyond doubt, but it was believed that Edwards was evaluating the airplane's stall characteristics, exceeded its maximum permissible speed while recovering from a stall and pulled up sharply, causing the wings to fold upward and break off. Despite the accident, the USAF gave Northrop a letter of intent for thirty RB-49A reconnaissance aircraft, modified for longer range. In November, the USAF announced that ten uncompleted YB-35s would be completed as RB-35B jet reconnaissance aircraft.

By the end of the year the entire program had been canceled. Thirty years later, the eighty-five-year-old Jack Northrop said in a television interview that the ax had fallen because Northrop would not agree to Air Force Secretary Stuart Symington's proposal that his company be merged into Convair. Jack Northrop alleged that the proposal was

A less successful Northrop venture was the barrel-like XP-56 fighter, a tailless type rather than a true flying wing. Control diffi- *culties were not resolved before the entire project was rendered obsolete by the jet age.* Jay Miller/Aerofax

made at a private house in Los Angeles. When he asked about alternatives, he said, Symington responded, "You'll be damned sorry if you don't." After negotiations between Northrop and Convair got nowhere, the production contract was terminated. Symington (who, at the time of this writing, is the only living participant at the alleged meeting) denies making such statements.

The Air Force had practical reasons for preferring other aircraft to the Northrop flying wings. Designed in 1941, the Northrop aircraft were designed to carry their bombload in several bays spread across the span. The largest single bomb that they could carry was the 4,000 pound type. But early USAF atomic bombs were based on the implosion-type Fat Man weapon which had been dropped on Nagasaki. Weighing 10,000 pounds and measuring sixty inches in diameter, they were too large to fit in the B-35 or B-49 without considerable redesign. Smaller weapons were only in the early study phase by the time the B-49 contract was canceled. However, the Boeing B-47 (which was eventually selected as the first jet strategic bomber and reconnaissance aircraft) was of later origin than the B-49 and was designed around existing A-bombs. The B-36, with its freight-car-sized bomb bay, could carry the monster MK17, the first US thermonuclear weapon.

Jack Northrop, creator of the US Flying Wing, in front of the first XB-35. Shortly before his death in 1981, Jack Northrop was granted a high-level security clearance, so *that he could be told about the new flying-wing bomber that would bear his name.* Northrop

Project Yehudi

The visual detectability of an aircraft can be reduced by the correct use of camouflage paint, but (under some conditions) it can be much more greatly diminished by the apparently crazy concept of mounting lights on the airframe. This was the secret of Project Yehudi, carried out in the early forties by the US Navy.

The Navy found that its patrol planes were failing to catch submarines because the crews could not see their quarry—black or gray against a dark-gray sea—until long after the submarine commander had seen the airplane—a black dot against a light-gray sky.

None of the many paint schemes seemed to solve the problem. Navy researchers realized that it was not the contrast in *tone* between the aircraft and the sky which made it stand out, but the contrast in *luminance;* the sky emitted more light energy than the aircraft. The U-boat skipper's eye was not seeing the airplane, but the difference between a radiant sky and a merely reflecting object.

Project Yehudi changed that situation. Lights were fitted on the noses and wings of Navy Liberators and Avengers, so that their intensity could be varied according to the brightness of the sky behind them. By all accounts, it worked. The distance at which the aircraft was visible was sharply reduced, so that a U-boat commander would have no time to close hatches and dive before his own craft could be seen. However, Yehudi appeared at just about the same time as ASV (air-to-surface-vessel) radar was developed. With ASV, patrol aircraft could detect submarines well beyond visual range, the need for Yehudi disappeared, and Project Yehudi itself vanished for almost four decades.

Yehudi has resurfaced for some specific applications. F-16s may have been tested with Yehudi lights in their deep, shadowed ventral inlets, which may actually be the first part of the airplane that an adversary sees. But strategic bombing is the least visual form of air combat, and it is likely that the B-2 gets by on its naturally slender profile and dark gray paint.

The B-2 industrial team

A program as large as the B-2 employs more than 30,000 people and hundreds of subcontractors. A partial list of these companies was released in 1988 by the USAF. Although their roles in the program were not specified, the locations at which the work was being done were identified, and it is possible to draw some inferences from the nonclassified work which is undertaken at the same locations.

Major team members

Northrop is the prime contractor and system integrator, responsible to the USAF for the performance of the entire aircraft, including its electronic systems, and for the performance of all the other contractors. This activity is centered on Northrop's B-2 Division at Pico Rivera, California. Northrop's main associates are Boeing Advanced Technology and LTV Aircraft Products Group.

A unit of the Boeing Company, Boeing Advanced Technology was "spun off" in 1986 from the former Boeing Military Airplane Company (BMAC). It consists of the Seattle-based portions of BMAC, including Boeing's shares of the B-2 and Lockheed YF-22A programs. Its role on the B-2 reportedly includes the manufacture of the outer wings. LTV Aircraft Products Group, based in Dallas, Texas, produces various specialized assemblies, possibly including parts of the engine installation. Unlike subcontractors on other aircraft programs, Boeing and LTV have apparently had detail design responsibility for the components they build, and deliver them fully "plumbed" (equipped with subsystems) to Palmdale.

General Electric's Aircraft Engine Group, which makes the F118 engine at Evendale, Ohio. Engines are usually "government-furnished equipment" (GFE), and the engine maker reports directly to the B-2 System Project Office (SPO) at Wright-Patterson AFB.

Radar and main avionics systems

Hughes Radar Systems Group, Los Angeles, California. Primarily a producer of advanced airborne radars. Hughes builds the B-2's radar.

General Electric's Aircraft Control Systems Department, Binghamton, New York. A developer of advanced flight control systems for aircraft such as the F-18 fighter and the V-22 tilt-rotor, and a leader in the development of integrated propulsion and flight-control systems. GE presumably does the same for the B-2.

Kearfott Guidance and Navigation Company, Little Falls, New Jersey. Specialist in high-precision inertial navigation equipment for strategic aircraft.

Honeywell Military Avionics Division, Minneapolis, Minnesota. Producer of the radar altimeter set (RAS), which must be of unusual design in order to provide accurate altitude data (essential for weapon delivery) without betraying the bomber's position.

Allied-Signal Aerospace Corporation, Teterboro, New Jersey. Three Allied-Signal units operate at this location, but the most likely of these to be involved in the B-2 is the Flight Systems Division, which specializes in advanced cockpit display systems.

Electronic warfare (EW)

Raytheon Electromagnetic Systems Division, Goleta, California. The only company on the published list of subcontractors with a strong interest in active jamming systems, Raytheon should be a major participant in the EW system. (Northrop's own ECM unit may also be involved, however.)

Honeywell, Wilmington, Massachusetts. Although this unit's activities have been transferred to other Honeywell plants in the region, its main products were threat warning systems.

Sanders Associates, Nashua, New Hampshire. This Lockheed unit has a wide range of EW capabilities, producing EW displays for the B-1 and numerous electronic surveillance devices.

Other contractors

Link Flight Simulation Corporation, Binghamton, New York. Produces the training system for the B-2, including simulated cockpits, advanced computer-generated image systems and software.

Boeing Military Airplanes, Wichita, Kansas. The other half of the former BMAC, Boeing Military Airplanes builds the Advanced Applications Rotary Launchers.

Unisys, Eagan, Minnesota. Major supplier of high-power airborne computers and signal processors.

Fairchild Communications and Electronics, Germantown, Maryland. A specialist in database-type systems and real-time image interpretation.

Miltope Corporation, Melville, New York. Specializes in rugged mass storage devices (such as magnetic and optical disk drives) for use in military air, land, sea and space vehicles.

Reference sources

Chapter 1: The survivable bomber

Airship raids. *Airships*, Henry Beaubois (London, Macdonald & Jane's, 1974).

Gotha attacks. *Bomber Command*, Max Hastings (London, Michael Joseph, 1979).

Bomber regulation. *The Shadow of the Bomber*, Uri Bialer (London, Royal Historical Society, 1980).

Pre-war bombing experience. *Bomber Command*, Max Hastings.

US bomber development. *The Development of the Heavy Bomber, 1918-1944* (US Air Force Air University, Historical Division, August 1951).

RAF campaign. *Bomber Command*, Max Hastings.

Electronic warfare. *Instruments of Darkness*, Alfred Price (London, Macdonald & Jane's, 1977).

B-29 origins. *The Superfortress is Born*, Thomas Collison (New York, Duell, Sloan & Pearce, 1945).

Mosquito capabilities. *Mosquito*, Bill Sweetman (London, Jane's, 1981).

LeMay and the 21st Command. *Iron Eagle*, Thomas M. Coffey (New York, Crown, 1986).

Britain's nuclear bombers. *V-Force*, Andrew Brookes (London, Jane's, 1982).

B-52 redesign. *Vision: The Story of Boeing*, Harold Mansfield (New York, Popular Library, 1966).

Snark. *Northrop: An Aeronautical History*, Fred Anderson (Los Angeles, Northrop Corporation, 1976).

Strategic Air Command. *Strategic Air Command: People, Aircraft and Missiles*, ed. Norman Polmar (Annapolis, Nautical & Aviation Publishing Company, 1979).

Bomb development. *US Nuclear Weapons*, Chuck Hansen (New York, Orion/Aerofax, 1988).

B-58. *Convair B-58*, Jay Miller (Arlington, TX, Aerofax, 1985).

B-70. *North American B-70 Valkyrie*, Steve Pace (Fallbrook, Aero Publishers, 1982).

F-111. *Modern Fighting Aircraft–F-111*, Bill Gunston (London, Salamander, 1984).

B-1 evolution. *Modern Fighting Aircraft–B-1B*, Mike Spick (London, Salamander, 1986).

SAC force changes. *Strategic Air Command*, Polmar.

Chapter 2: Vanishing tricks

Horten flying wings. *Nurflugel*, Reimar Horten and Peter F. Selinger (Graz, Austria, H. Weishaupt Verlag, 1985).

Transparent aircraft experiments. "So, What's New About Stealth?" Peter M. Grosz (*Air International*, September 1986).

Schornfeinsteger. "Electromagnetic Wave Absorbers," William H. Emerson (*IEEE Transactions on Antennas and Propagation*, July 1973).

Watson-Watt. *Stealth Warplanes*, Bill Gunston (London, Osprey, 1988).

MIT work. "Electromagnetic Wave Absorbers," Emerson.

U-2. *Lockheed U-2*, Jay Miller (Arlington, TX, Aerofax 1983)

SR-71. *Development of the SR-71*, Clarence L. Johnson (Lockheed-California, 1982) and interviews.

Ryan reconnaissance drones. *Lightning Bugs*, William A. Wagner (Fallbrook, Aero Publishers, 1982).

YO-3. *X-Planes*, Jay Miller (Specialty Press, 1982).

Linebacker strikes. *Air War–Vietnam, introduction by Drew Middleton (New York, Bobbs-Merrill, 1979)*.

XB-47 "sacred airplane," *The Leading Edge*, Walter J. Boyne (Smithsonian 1986).

Chapter 3: The Gigabuck Zone

B-1 development. *Wild Blue Yonder*, Nick Kotz (New York, Pantheon, 1988).

Cruise missile evolution. "The Cruise Missile," Doug Richardson (*Flight International*, October 1, 1977).

Carter's B-1 decision. *Wild Blue Yonder*, Nick Kotz.

SAC view of B-1 in 1979. Letter from Gen. Ellis of Rep. Bob Carr of Michigan, quoted in *Aviation Week*, June 16, 1980.

Reagan's B-1 decision. *Wild Blue Yonder*, Nick Kotz.

Black budget. Tim Weiner, (*Philadelphia Inquirer*, January 1987).

Likely delays in B-2 production. "Full-Scale Output of Stealth Bomber Is Likely to Be Delayed Well into 1990s," Andy Pasztor and Eileen White Read (*Wall Street Journal*, December 8, 1988).

Chapter 4: Under the skin

Northrop quotation. *35th Wilbur Wright Memorial Lecture to the Royal Aeronautical Society*, John K. Northrop (London, RAeS 1947). This lecture is reproduced in full as an appendix to Jack Northrop and the Flying Wing, Ted Coleman with Robert Wenkam (New York, Paragon House, 1988).

Radar-range basics. *Radar Cross-Section Lectures*, Allen E. Fuhs (New York, American Institute of Aeronautics and Astronautics, 1985).

Comparative RCS. *Radar Cross-Section Lectures*, Fuhs.

YB-49 flights against coastal radars. *Jack Northrop and the Flying Wing*, Coleman.

Flying-wing history. *Winged Wonders—The Story of the Flying Wings*, E. T. Wooldridge (Washington DC, Smithsonian Institution, 1983).

Flying-wing advantages. *Wilbur Wright Lecture*, Northrop.

X-4. *X-Planes*, Miller, and lecture by Scott Crossfield.

Artificial stability. *Wilbur Wright Lecture*, Northrop.

Computer-integrated manufacturing. *Aircraft Manufacture–The Next Generation* and *B-2 Three-Dimensional Database videos* (Los Angeles, Northrop Corporation, 1988).

B-49 weight. *Wilbur Wright Lecture*, Northrop.

Lockheed spanloader studies. *Review of Unconventional Aircraft Design Concepts*, Roy H. Lange, Lockheed-Georgia (Journal of Aircraft, May 1988).

B-52 weights and performance. *Strategic Air Command*, Polmar.

Chapter 5: Weapons of Armageddon

History of nuclear doctrine. *The Evolution of Nuclear Strategy*, Lawrence Freedman (New York, St. Martin's Press, 1981).

Soviet civil defense efforts. *Deep Black*, William E. Burrows (New York, Random House, 1986).

SICBM and Peacekeeper RG details. Speakers at Air Force Association symposium on strategic forces, Omaha, June 1988.

Soviet mobile ICBMs. *Soviet Military Power* (Washington DC, Department of Defense, 1988).

Milstar "warfighter's comsat." Lt. Gen. Aloysius G. Casey, commander, Space Division, Air Force Systems Command, at Omaha AFA symposium.

Hard targets. "Defense Dept. Plans to Study Earth-Penetrating Nuclear Weapons," John D. Morrocco (*Aviation Week*, June 8, 1987).

Withdrawal of MK53s from retirement. *US Nuclear Weapons*, Hansen.

British heavy bombs. *The Dam Busters*, Paul Brickhill (London, Pan, 1964).

BLU-109. "Air-to-surface weapons—US programs," Bill Sweetman (*International Defense Review*, May 1986).

Chapter 6: Stealth tactics

Information on Soviet systems. *Soviet Military Power*, DoD; *Jane's All the World's Aircraft 1987-88* (London, Jane's Information Group); *MiGs*, Bill Sweetman (London, Salamander, 1985).

Soviet fighter-support truck and maintenance philosophy. *Information* *from Richard D. Ward, General Dynamics.*

B83 data. *US Nuclear Weapons,* Hansen.

ASARS-2 performance. Donald G. Latham, then assistant secretary of defense for C31, quoted in *Air Force Magazine.*

Conventional tactics. SAC officers at Air Force Association symposium on tactical air warfare, Orlando, January 1987.

Resonance effects. Radar cross-section lectures, Fuhs.

Soviet radar wavelengths. *The International Countermeasures Handbook* (Palo Alto, EW Communications, 1985).

Bistatic radar. Briefing to author from ITT-Gilfillan.

Anti-Stealth radar. US Patent application by Professor Henning Harmuth of the Catholic University of America, Washington DC, 1986.

Appendix 2—The Flying Wing Controversy

Northrop's claims against Symington are summarized in *Jack Northrop and the Flying Wing,* by Ted Coleman. Another view is given in *A Synopsis of Flying Wing Development, 1908-53,* by Richard P. Hallion (History Office, Air Force Flight Test Center, 1986).

Index